Charles H. Gabriel

Sifted Wheat

A collection of songs for Sunday schools, young people's societies, devotional and revival meetings

Charles H. Gabriel

Sifted Wheat
A collection of songs for Sunday schools, young people's societies, devotional and revival meetings

ISBN/EAN: 9783337182069

Printed in Europe, USA, Canada, Australia, Japan

Cover: Foto ©Lupo / pixelio.de

More available books at **www.hansebooks.com**

A Collection of Songs

FOR

Sunday Schools, Young People's Societies Devotional and Revival Meetings

BY

CHAS. H. GABRIEL

LORENZ & COMPANY, Publishers
DAYTON, OHIO

Copyright, 1898, by E. S. Lorenz

PUBLISHERS' PREFACE

The work of Mr. Gabriel as a composer of popular Sunday-school music is too highly appreciated by the general public to need any praise from us. We are sure that this volume of songs will add to his reputation and open a wider field of usefulness to his prolific and successful pen. We join with him in hoping that it will bring good cheer and sunshine as well as spiritual inspiration and profit wherever it is introduced

SIFTED WHEAT.

No. 1. WATCHING BY THE CROSS.

E. E. Hewitt.   E. S. Lorenz.

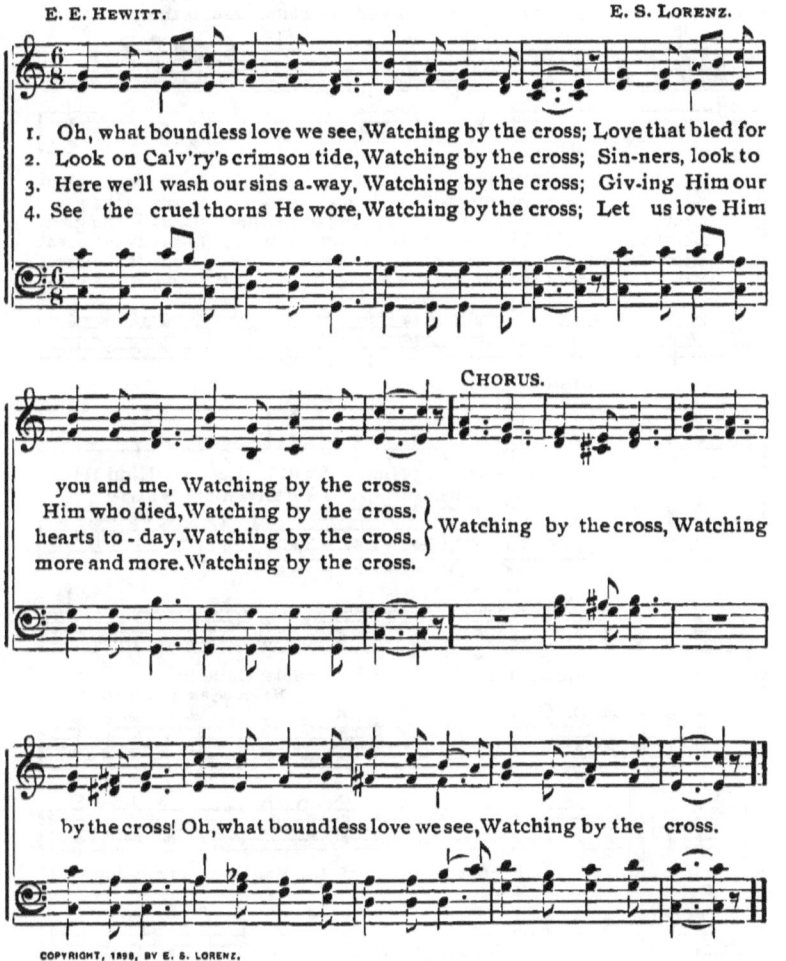

1. Oh, what boundless love we see, Watching by the cross; Love that bled for you and me, Watching by the cross.
2. Look on Calv'ry's crimson tide, Watching by the cross; Sin-ners, look to Him who died, Watching by the cross.
3. Here we'll wash our sins a-way, Watching by the cross; Giv-ing Him our hearts to-day, Watching by the cross.
4. See the cruel thorns He wore, Watching by the cross; Let us love Him more and more, Watching by the cross.

CHORUS.

Watching by the cross, Watching by the cross! Oh, what boundless love we see, Watching by the cross.

Copyright, 1898, by E. S. Lorenz.

Tell the Story.

ran - somed sing, 'Till the world.... the truth em-brace..........
ransomed ev-er sing, Tell the sto - ry 'till the world the truth embrace.

No. 5. I'M SO GLAD THAT I LOVE JESUS.

J. E. H.   Arr. by J. E. Hazen.

1. I'm so glad that I love Je - sus, For He is so dear to me;
2. I'm so glad that I love Je - sus, For I'm sure of one true Friend;
3. I'm so glad that I love Je - sus, For when comes the time to die,

I have found His love is sweet-er   Than all things of earth can be.
Thro' the shadows and the sunshine, He will love me to the end.
He will bear me in His bos-om   Safe-ly to His home on high.

Chorus.

I am so glad that Jesus I know; I am so glad, I do love Him so;

Rit.

I am so glad that Je-sus I know; I am so glad, I do love Him so.

COPYRIGHT, 1897, BY CHAS. H. GABRIEL.

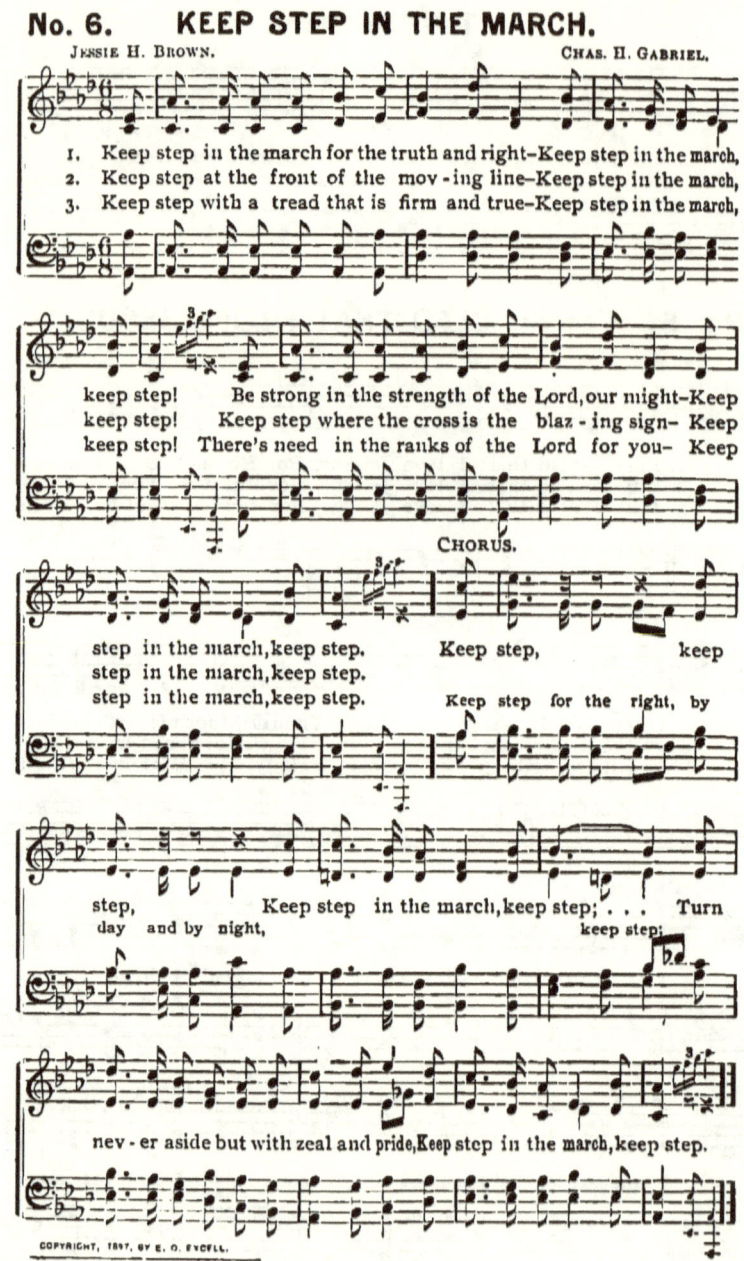

No. 14. SCATTER SEED.

J. L. MOORE.

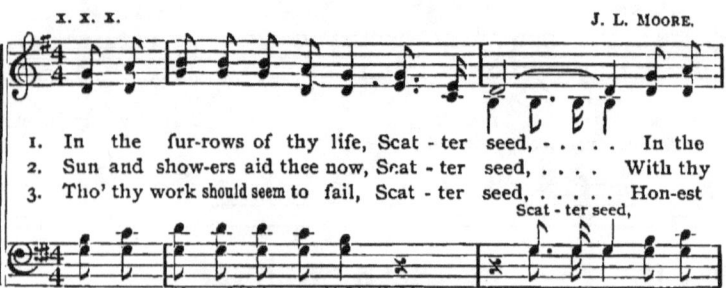

1. In the fur-rows of thy life, Scat-ter seed, — . . . . In the
2. Sun and show-ers aid thee now, Scat-ter seed, ... With thy
3. Tho' thy work should seem to fail, Scat-ter seed, ... Hon-est

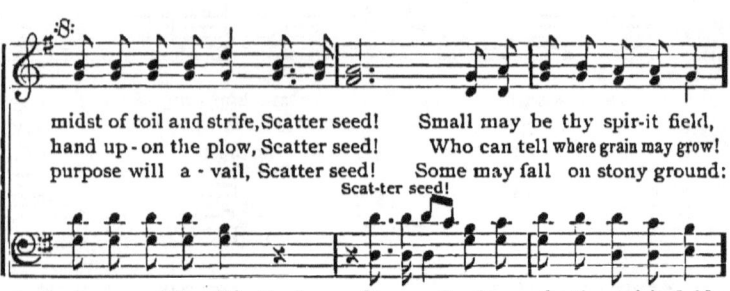

midst of toil and strife, Scatter seed! Small may be thy spir-it field,
hand up-on the plow, Scatter seed! Who can tell where grain may grow!
purpose will a-vail, Scatter seed! Some may fall on stony ground:

D. S.—furrows of thy life, Scatter seed! Small may be thy spirit field,

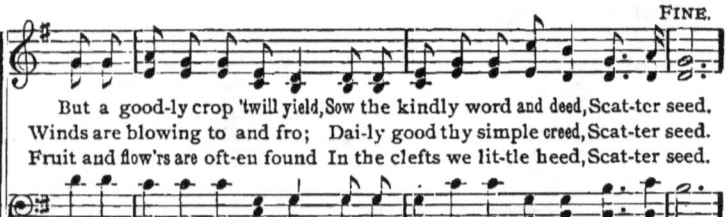

But a good-ly crop 'twill yield, Sow the kindly word and deed, Scat-ter seed.
Winds are blowing to and fro; Dai-ly good thy simple creed, Scat-ter seed.
Fruit and flow'rs are oft-en found In the clefts we lit-tle heed, Scat-ter seed.

But a good-ly crop 'twill yield, Sow the kindly word and deed, Scat-ter seed.

CHORUS. D. S.

Scat-ter seed, ... scat-ter seed; . . . . . In the
Scat-ter seed of good, yes, scat-ter, scat-ter seed;

COPYRIGHT, 1890, BY CHAS. H. GABRIEL.

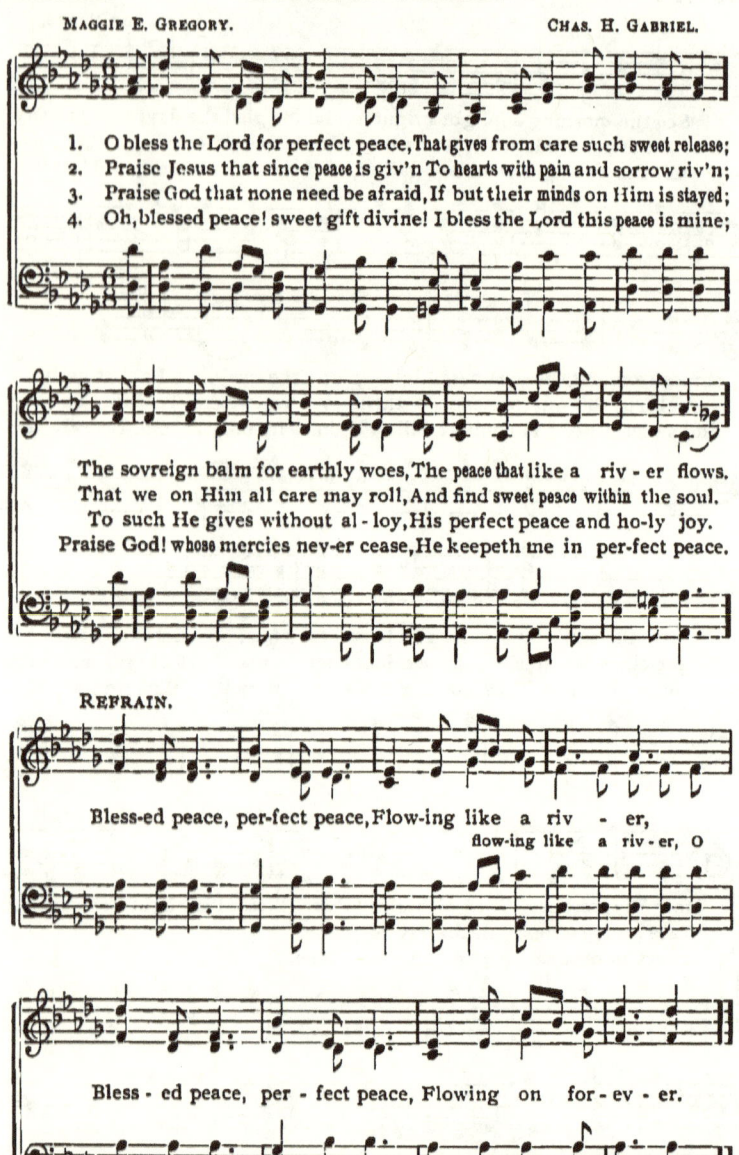

Onward, Christian Soldier.

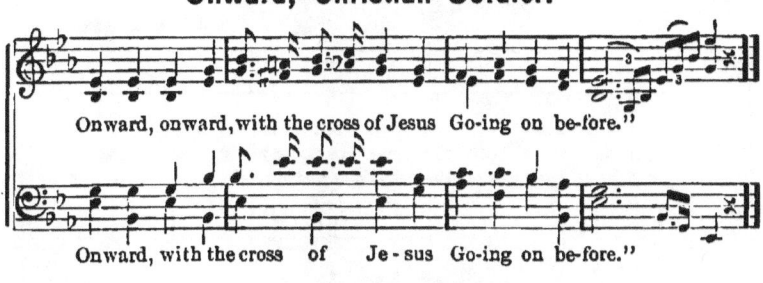

Onward, onward, with the cross of Jesus Going on before."

Onward, with the cross of Jesus Going on before."

No. 21. PRAISE HIM.

CHARLOTTE G. HOMER.   J. H. ROSECRANS.

1. Praise the Rock of our salvation, Come before Him with a song;
2. Praise the Rock of our salvation, Just and merciful is He,
3. Praise the Rock of our salvation, For His blood avails for sin!

For the Lord our God is holy,—Praises unto Him belong.
Strong and mighty to deliver,—Unto Him for refuge flee
At the gate of mercy standing, He invites the wand'rer in.

CHORUS.

Praise Him! praise Him! Sing aloud in exultation!

Praise Him! praise Him! Praise the Rock of our salvation!

COPYRIGHT, 1894, BY CHAS. H. GABRIEL.

No. 26. SOMETHING TO BE DONE.

M. D. CHELLIS.   CHAS. H. GABRIEL.

1. There's a bat-tle to be fought, A vict-'ry to be gained;
2. There's an en-e-my a-broad, So sub-tile and so strong,
3. We're re-cruit-ing for the ranks, For years and years to come,

There's a coun-try to be saved, A host from sin re-claimed.
That the con-flict must be fierce, The strug-gle must be long.
That our num-ber may not fail Ere tri-umph shall be won.

CHORUS.
Yes, there's something to be done! Something to be done! Let us then no longer waste the precious moments as they fly! Oh, there's something to be done! there's something to be done! There are precious souls to save, There's something to be done!

COPYRIGHT, 1896, BY CHAS. H. GABRIEL.

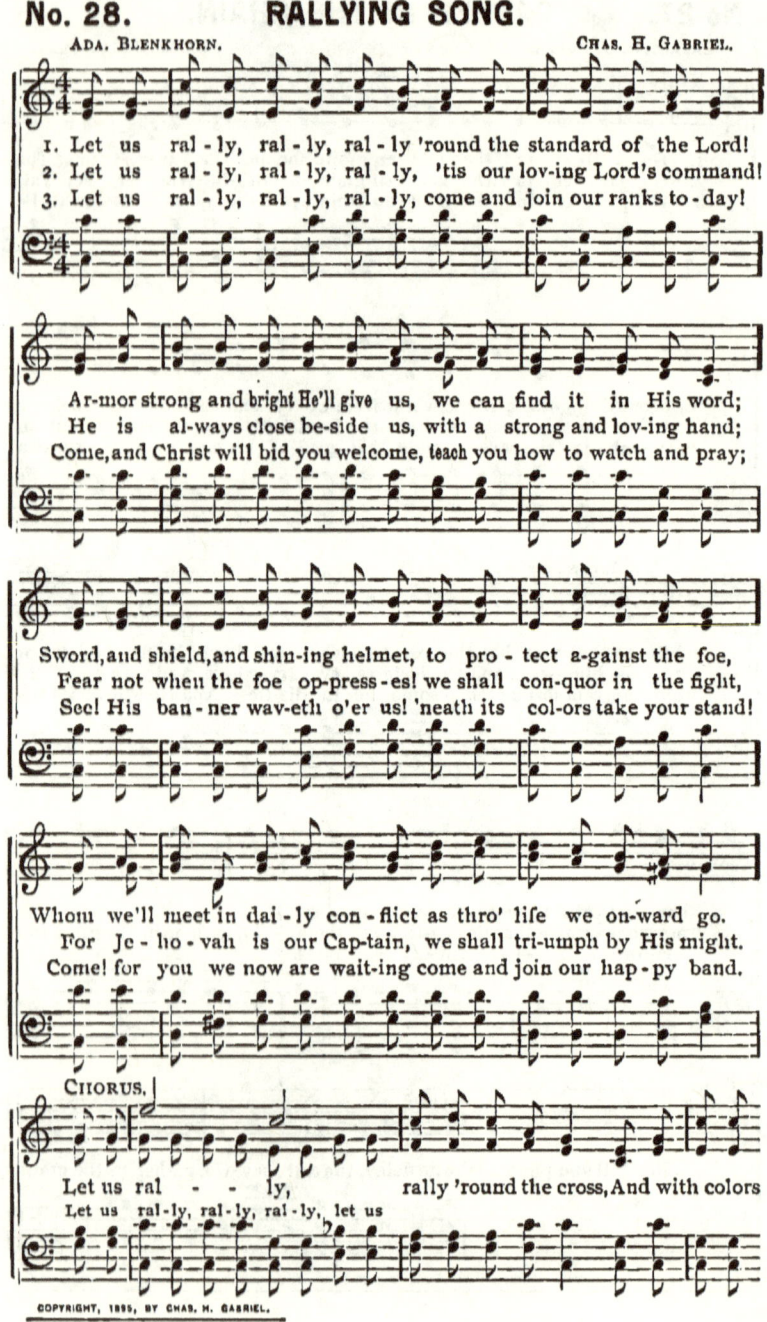

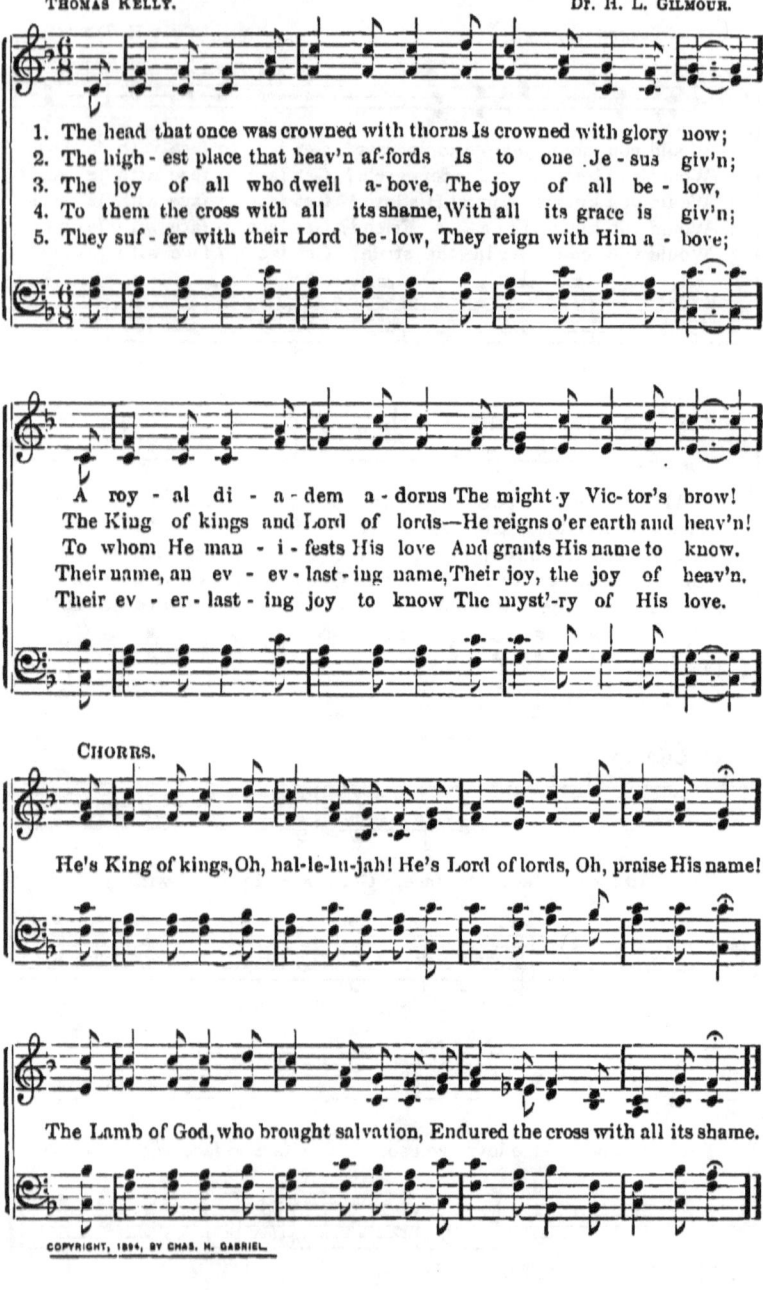

No. 36. THE BRIDEGROOM COMETH.

IDA M. BUDD.   CHAS. H. GABRIEL.

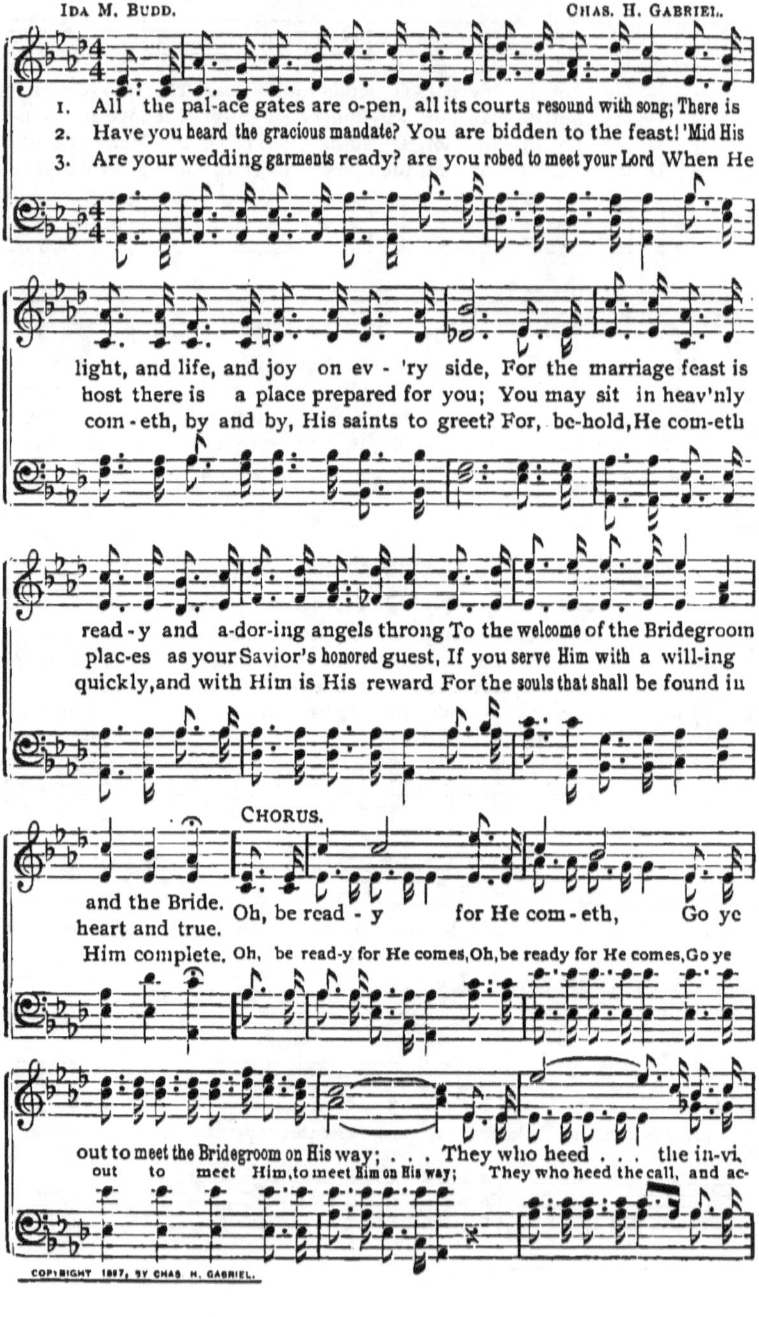

1. All the pal-ace gates are o-pen, all its courts resound with song; There is
2. Have you heard the gracious mandate? You are bidden to the feast! 'Mid His
3. Are your wedding garments ready? are you robed to meet your Lord When He

light, and life, and joy on ev-'ry side, For the marriage feast is
host there is a place prepared for you; You may sit in heav'nly
com-eth, by and by, His saints to greet? For, be-hold, He com-eth

read-y and a-dor-ing angels throng To the welcome of the Bridegroom
plac-es as your Savior's honored guest, If you serve Him with a will-ing
quickly, and with Him is His reward For the souls that shall be found in

CHORUS.

and the Bride.   Oh, be read-y for He com-eth,   Go ye
heart and true.
Him complete.   Oh, be read-y for He comes, Oh, be ready for He comes, Go ye

out to meet the Bridegroom on His way; . . . They who heed . . . the in-vi-
out to meet Him, to meet Him on His way; They who heed the call, and ac-

COPYRIGHT 1897, BY CHAS. H. GABRIEL.

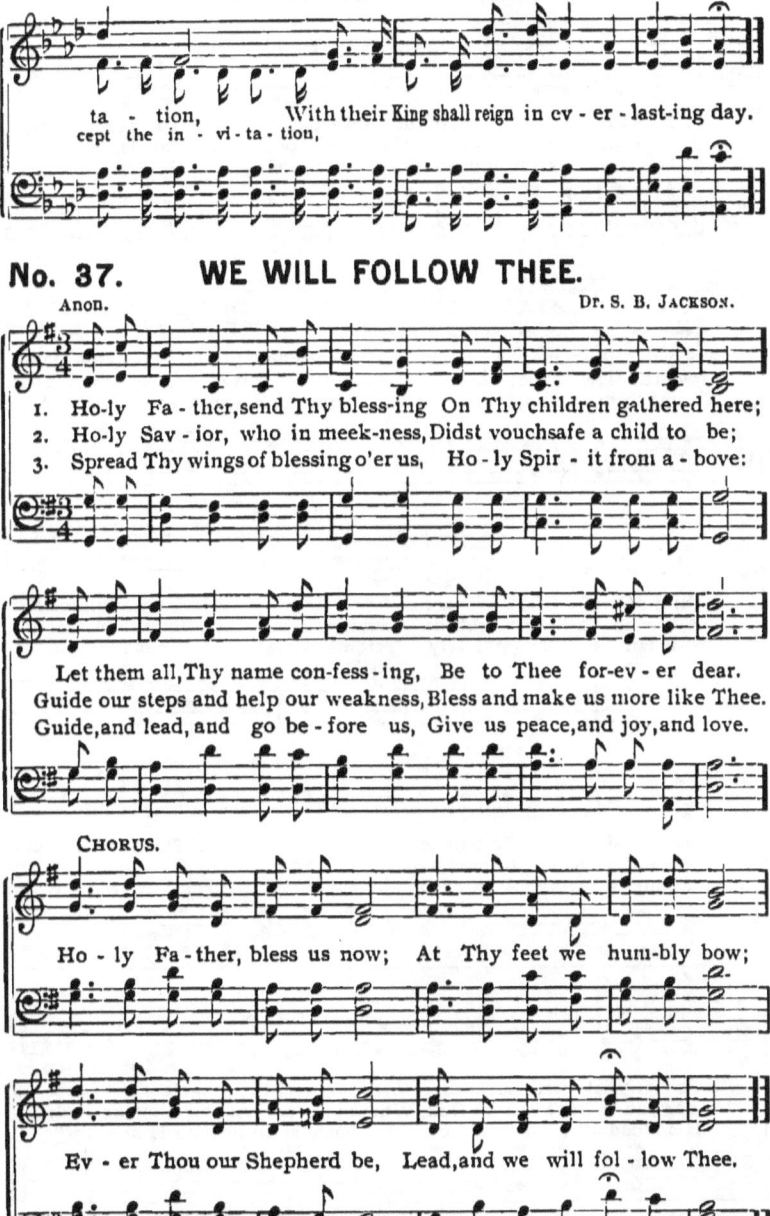

Happy in My Savior.

hap-py, so ver-y hap-py in Je - sus all the day!
hap-py, oh, so ver-y hap-py in Je-sus, hap-py all the day!

No. 49. TURN THEE, BROTHER.

J. F. CLARK.   ADOLPH JESREAL.

1. Broth-er hast thou wan-dered far From thy Father's hap-py home,
2. Is a might-y fam-ine now In thy heart and in thy soul?
3. He can heal thy bitt-'rest wound, He thy gentlest prayer can hear;

With thy-self and God at war? Turn thee, brother; homeward come.
Dis-con-tent up-on thy brow? Turn thee; God will make thee whole.
Seek Him, for He may be found; Call up-on Him; He is near.

CHORUS.

Turn thee, broth - - er; homeward come..... He is waiting to for-
Turn thee, brother, homeward come, homeward come, homeward come,

give, He is wait - ing; wait - - - ing to for - give.
He is waiting to forgive; wait-ing, He is wait-ing to for - give.

COPYRIGHT, 1897, BY CHAS. H. GABRIEL.

Loyal and True.

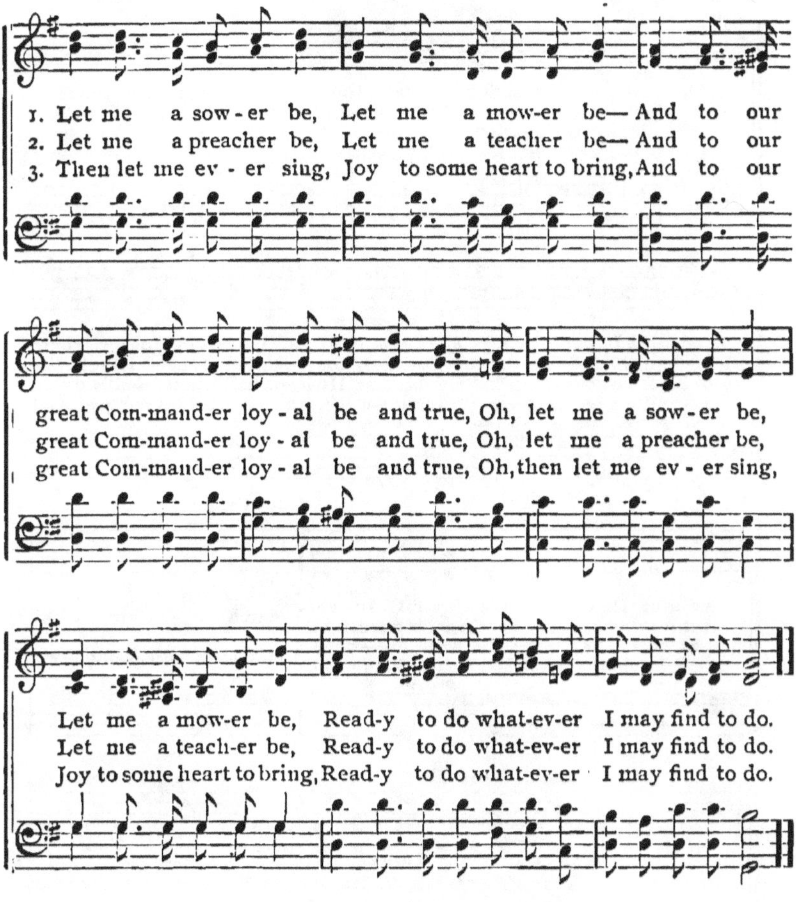

1. Let me a sow-er be, Let me a mow-er be— And to our
2. Let me a preacher be, Let me a teacher be— And to our
3. Then let me ev-er sing, Joy to some heart to bring, And to our

great Com-mand-er loy-al be and true, Oh, let me a sow-er be,
great Com-mand-er loy-al be and true, Oh, let me a preacher be,
great Com-mand-er loy-al be and true, Oh, then let me ev-er sing,

Let me a mow-er be, Read-y to do what-ev-er I may find to do.
Let me a teach-er be, Read-y to do what-ev-er I may find to do.
Joy to some heart to bring, Read-y to do what-ev-er I may find to do.

No. 51. THE LORD'S PRAYER. No. 1.

1. Our Father which art in heaven, hallowed | be Thy name, ‖Thy kingdom come, Thy will be done in | earth, as it | is in | heaven.
2. Give us this day our | daily | bread, ‖And forgive us our trespasses, as we forgive | them that | trespass a- | gainst us.
3. And lead us not into temptation, but deliver | us from | evil; ‖For Thine is the kingdom, and the power and the | glory for- | ever and | ever. ‖A- | men.

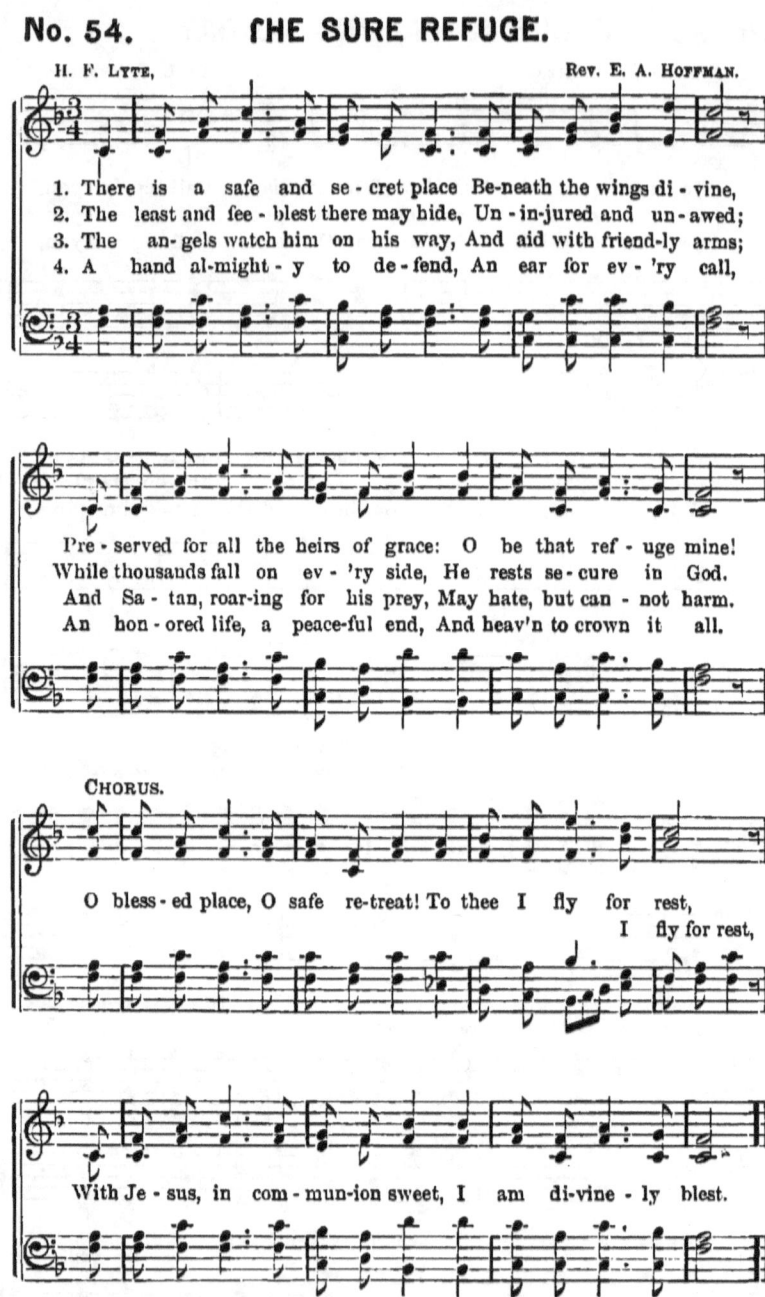

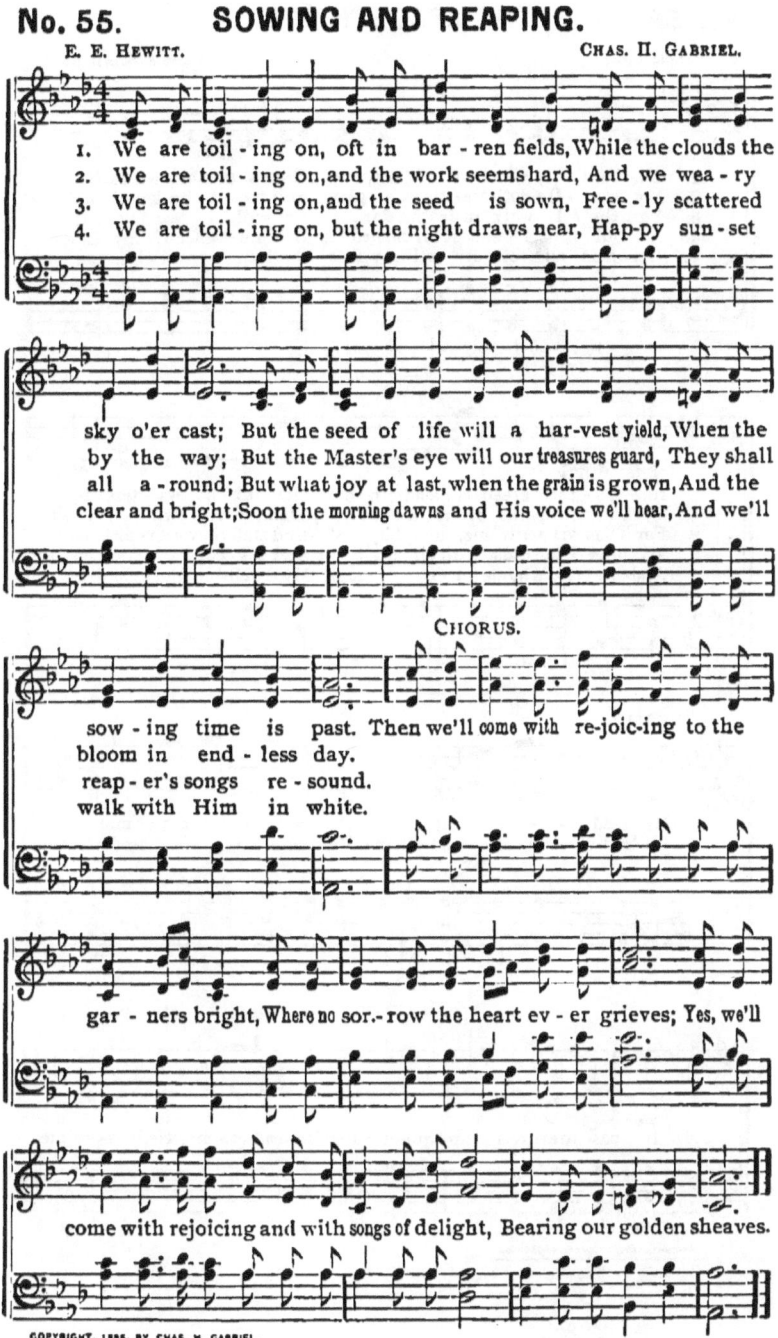

No. 57. O THE NEW BRIGHT CLIME.

Rev. H. G. Jackson, D. D.   Chas. H. Gabriel.

1. O the new bright clime of heav-en, Land of promise, Home of rest!
2. Friends from whom 'twas death to sever, There again shall clasp the hand;
3. Christ who saved us by His dy-ing We shall see in tri-umph there;
4. With the ransom'd we'll a-dore Him, And His glo-rious prais-es sing;

There for mourning, joy is giv-en, Sweet re-lease to souls op-press'd.
There shall meet to dwell for-ev-er, In the ra-diant sum-mer land.
And with saints and an-gels vy-ing, All His wondrous grace de-clare.
With arch-an-gels bow be-fore Him, Christ the ev-er-last-ing King.

Chorus.

Sing, sing of heav'n, Land of promise, Home of rest.
Sing of heav'n, O sing of heav'n,

Sing, sing of heav'n, Land of promise, Home of rest.
Sing of heav'n, O sing of heav'n,

COPYRIGHT, 1894, BY CHAS. H. GABRIEL.

No. 58. A PERFECT HEART.

Charles Wesley.
Frederic H. Pease.

1. O for a heart to praise my God, A heart from sin set free!
2. A heart resigned, submissive, meek, My great Redeemer's throne,
3. O for a lowly, contrite heart, Believing, true and clean,
4. A heart in ev-'ry tho't renewed, And full of love divine;

A heart that always feels Thy blood, So freely spilt for me.
Where only Christ is heard to speak, Where Jesus reigns alone.
Which neither life nor death can part From Him that dwells within.
Perfect, and right, and pure and good, A copy, Lord, of Thine.

Chorus.

Thy nature, gracious Lord, impart; Come quickly from above;

Write Thy new name upon my heart, Thy new, best name of Love.

Copyright, 1894, by Chas. H. Gabriel.

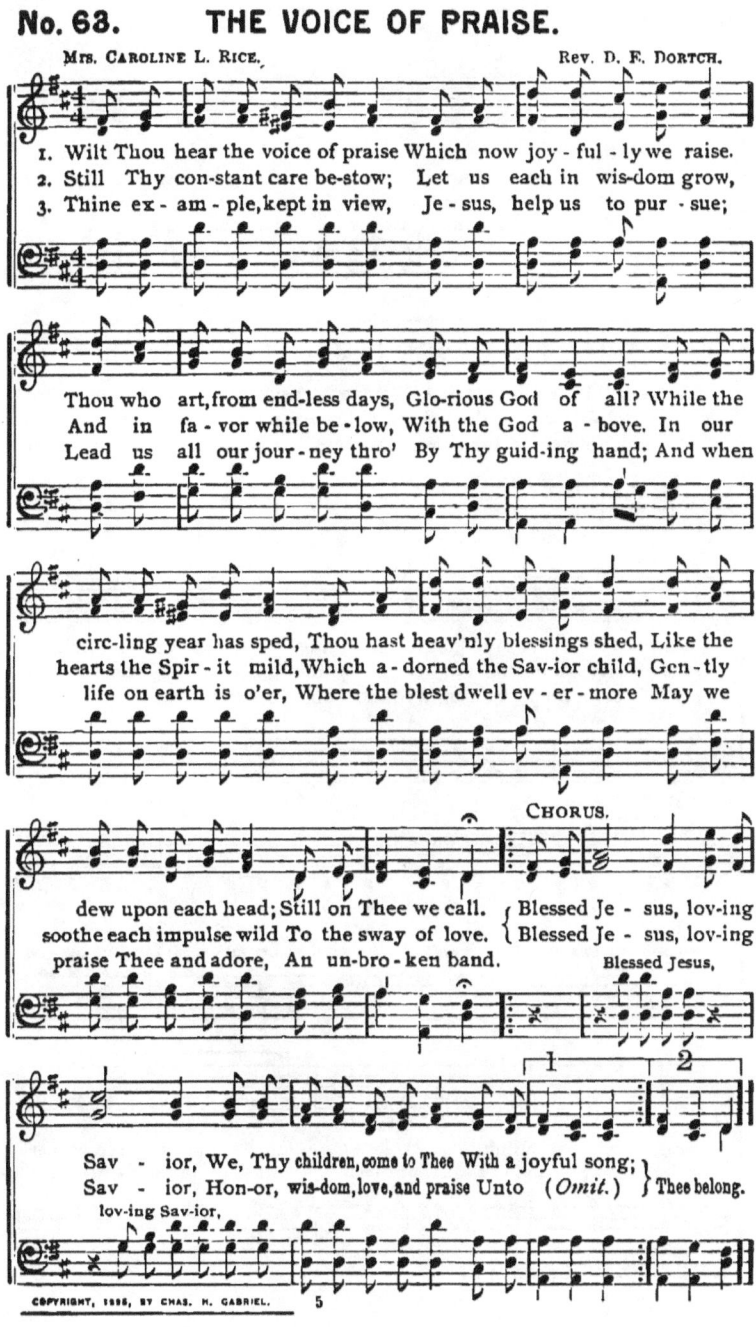

...forward, While the bells of glory sweetly, sweetly chime.
For-ward, ev-er forward, While the bells of glo-ry sweet-ly chime.

No. 65. BLESSED JESUS.

CHAS. H. GABRIEL.

1. Bless-ed Je-sus, God's own child! Gen-tle Je-sus, meek and mild,
2. Own me, Je-sus, I am Thine; Let Thy love with-in me shine;
3. Heav'nly Guardian of my heart, May I from Thee nev-er part;

Great Thy beau-ty, great Thy love, Ho-ly Je-sus, Heav'nly Dove.
Help me to be free from sin, Pure with-out, and pure with-in.
Pre-cious Lov-er of my soul, Keep my life in Thy con-trol.

CHORUS.

Je-sus, dear Je-sus, In joy-ful lays we give Thee praise;

Je-sus, dear Je-sus, Thy chil-dren we would be.

COPYRIGHT, 1899, BY CHAS. H. GABRIEL.

No 66. SINCE JESUS DWELLS WITHIN.

REV. F. L. SNYDER. H. A. HENRY.

1. I now can sing redemption's song, Since Jesus dwells within;
2. I feel a joy that's all divine, Since Jesus dwells within;
3. I have a peace I can't express, Since Jesus dwells within!
4. I have a hope that's strong and bright, Since Jesus dwells within;

Thro' faith my soul is borne along, Since Jesus dwells within.
For I am His and He is mine, Since Jesus dwells within.
All thro' His blood and righteousness, Since Jesus dwells within.
No cloud to shade, but all is light, Since Jesus dwells within.

CHORUS.

Since Jesus dwells within, Since Jesus dwells within, There's
Jesus dwells, He dwells within,

constant vict-'ry in my soul Since Jesus dwells within.

COPYRIGHT, 1897, BY CHAS H GABRIEL

Glory for Me.

O that will be glory for me, ... Yes, that will be glory for me; ... Just to be glo-ry for me, be glo-ry for me;

No. 71. TRUST IT ALL WITH JESUS.

ADA BLENKHORN.   CHAS. H. GABRIEL.

1. Oh, pil-grim art thou wea-ry, Thine eyes with weeping dim?
2. Do bur-dens fall up-on you, More than you think your share?
3. Ye wea-ry, heav-y la-den'd, By grief and care op-press'd,

Go, tell it all to Je-sus, And trust it all with Him.
Go, take them to the Sav-ior; You'll find a sol-ace there.
Oh, seek the Christ who loves you, And He will give you rest.

CHORUS.

O trust it all with Je-sus, Trust it all with Je-sus,

Yes, trust it all with Je-sus, A faith-ful Friend He'll be.

COPYRIGHT, 1897, BY CHAS. H. GABRIEL.

No. 73. BE A GOLDEN SUNBEAM.

Isaac Naylor.
Chas. H. Gabriel.

1. Be a gold-en sun-beam, ra-di-ant and bright, Chasing from life's path-way sor-row's frowning night; With thy gold-en sun-light dry the dew-y tear, Scat-ter from the sad heart all its doubt and fear.
2. When the way is gloom-y, cheer it with a song,— Ban-ish mist and shad-ow as you march a-long; In the place of bri-ars, strew the fairest flow'rs, Wreathing brows with roses pluck'd from heav'nly bow'rs.
3. Be a gold-en sun-beam, bright, and pure, and fair; With thy smiles and son-nets light-en hu-man care; With the sweet-est mu-sic from the harp of love, Lure the sad and wea-ry to our home a-bove.

Chorus

{ Be a gold-en sun-beam, beau-ti-ful and bright, Scat-ter-ing
{ Be a gold-en sun-beam, joy-ful-ly and glad, Scat-ter-ing

clouds and darkness with thy shining light:
rays of sun-light .... when the way is sad.

Copyright, 1894, by Chas. H. Gabriel.

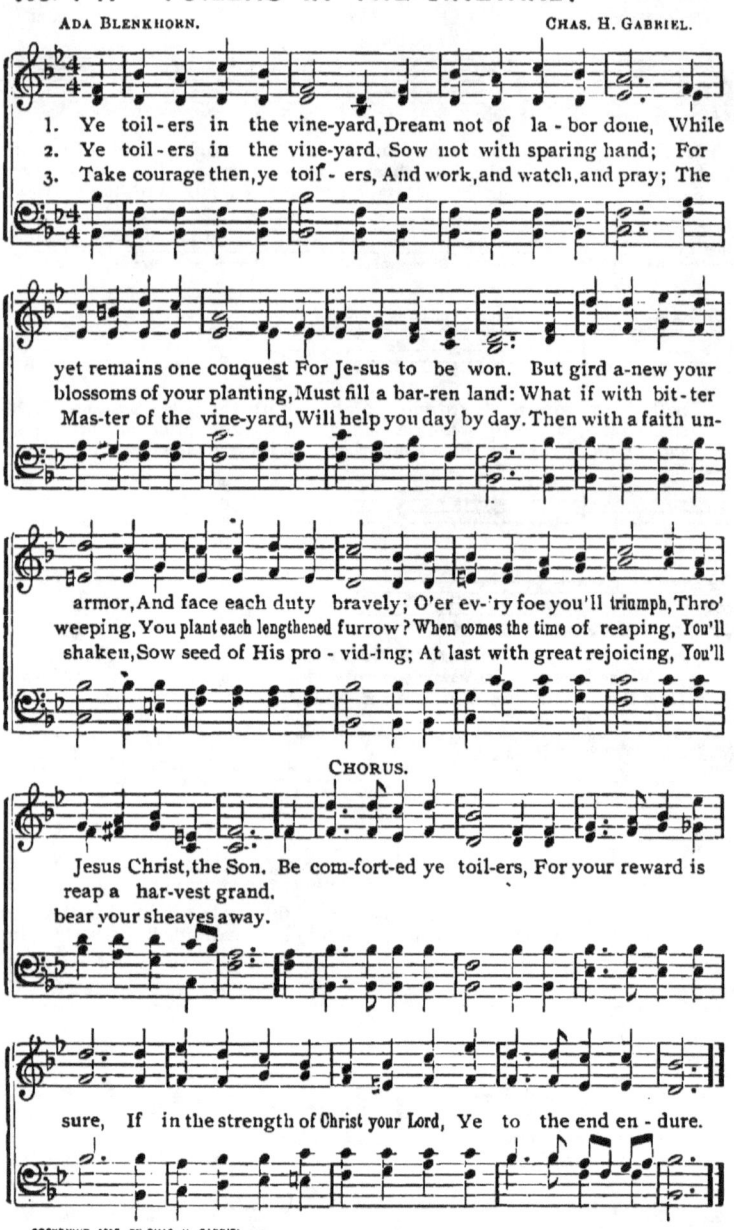

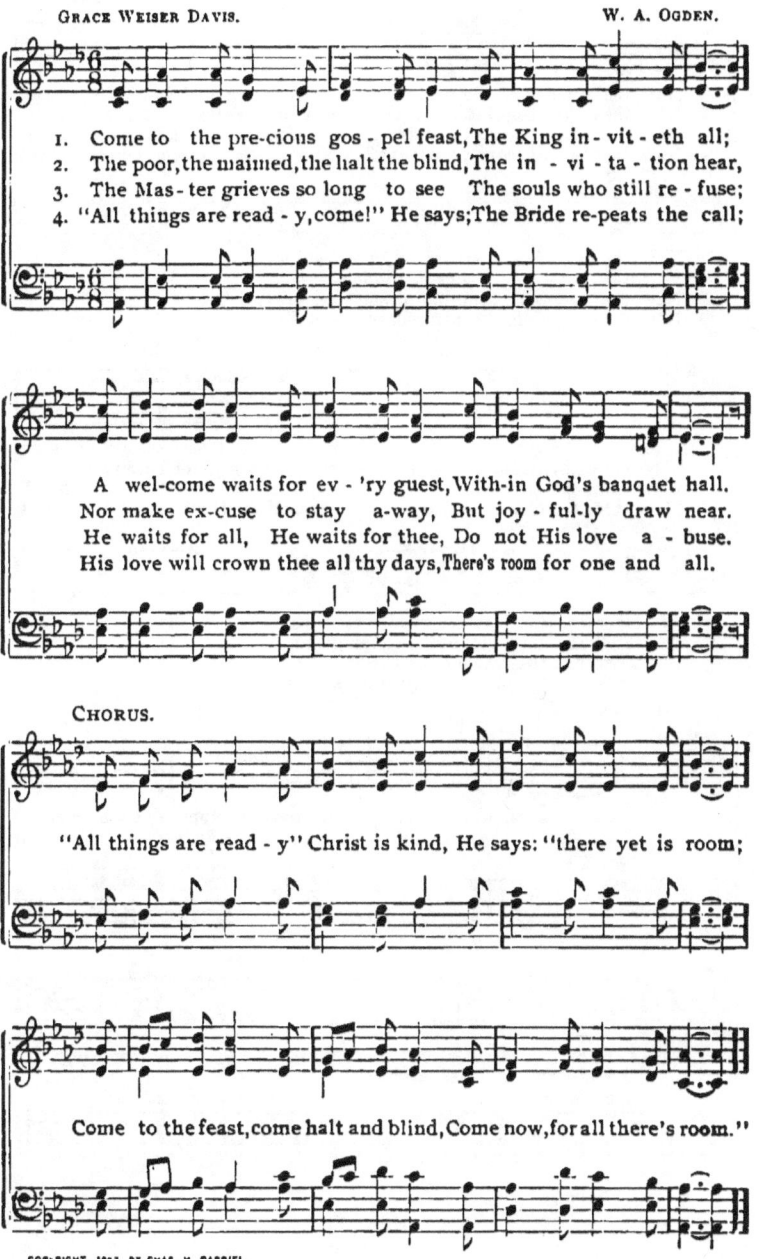

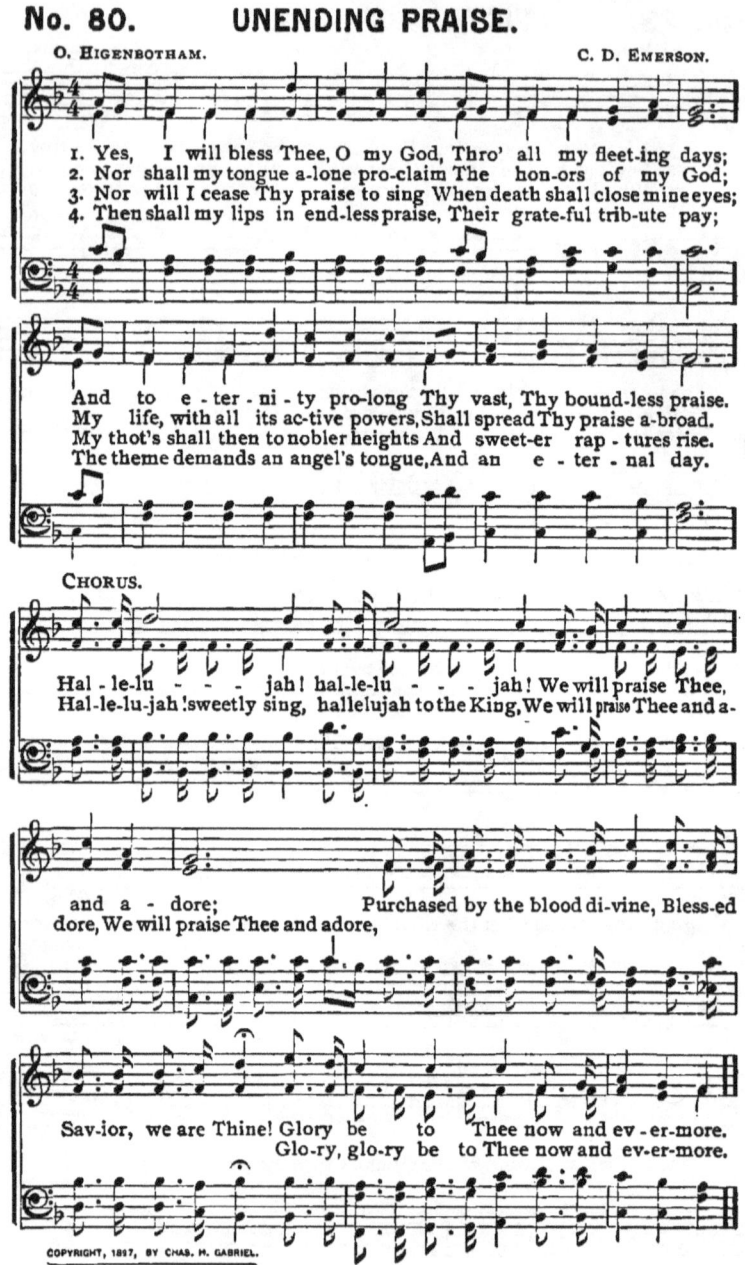

No. 82. JESUS LEADS THE WAY.

ADA BLENHORN.   CHAS. H. GABRIEL.

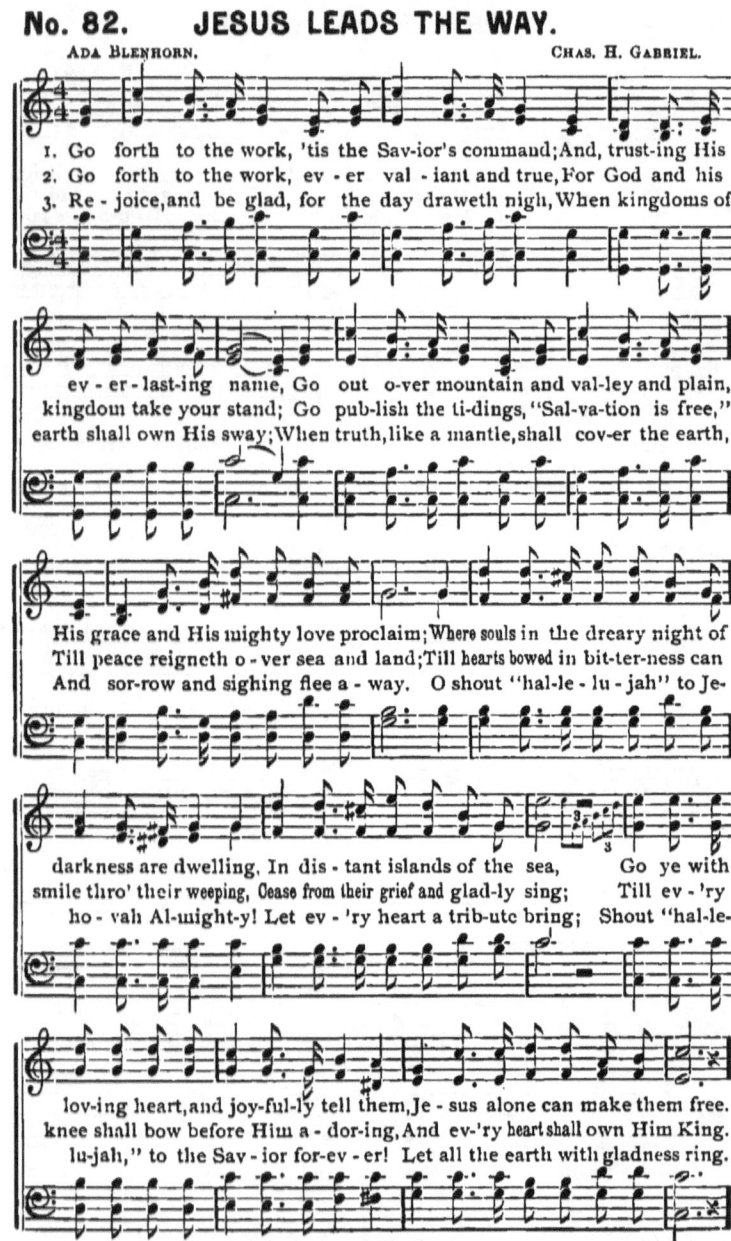

1. Go forth to the work, 'tis the Sav-ior's command; And, trust-ing His ev-er-last-ing name, Go out o-ver mountain and val-ley and plain, His grace and His mighty love proclaim; Where souls in the dreary night of darkness are dwelling, In dis-tant islands of the sea, Go ye with lov-ing heart, and joy-ful-ly tell them, Je-sus alone can make them free.

2. Go forth to the work, ev-er val-iant and true, For God and his kingdom take your stand; Go pub-lish the ti-dings, "Sal-va-tion is free," Till peace reigneth o-ver sea and land; Till hearts bowed in bit-ter-ness can smile thro' their weeping, Cease from their grief and glad-ly sing; Till ev-'ry knee shall bow before Him a-dor-ing, And ev-'ry heart shall own Him King.

3. Re-joice, and be glad, for the day draweth nigh, When kingdoms of earth shall own His sway; When truth, like a mantle, shall cov-er the earth, And sor-row and sighing flee a-way. O shout "hal-le-lu-jah" to Je-ho-vah Al-might-y! Let ev-'ry heart a trib-ute bring; Shout "hal-le-lu-jah," to the Sav-ior for-ev-er! Let all the earth with gladness ring.

COPYRIGHT, 1898, BY CHAS. H. GABRIEL.

The King's Highway.

children's voices sweet Swell the songs that cheer the pilgrims on their way.

No. 85. SHOUT THE TIDINGS.

D. M. C.   D. M. CHUTE.

1. Shout the tid-ings of sal - va-tion, Bear the mes-sage far and wide;
2. Shout the tid-ings of sal - va-tion, Sit not i - dly by the way;
3. Shout the tid-ings of sal - va-tion, Spread the word from shore to shore!

Spread the feast for ev - 'ry na-tion— Tell of Je - sus cru - ci - fied!
Heed the mes-sage of the Master:—"Go and work for me to - day."
Je - sus' mer-cy is un - measured, And His love a boundless store!

Chorus.

Hal - le - lu - jah for Je - sus! Shout the tid-ings a - gain!

Hal - le - lu - jah for Je - sus, Now and ev - er! A - men.

COPYRIGHT, 1893, BY CHAS. H. GABRIEL.

No. 88. HERE AM I.

ADA BLENKHORN.   Dr. S. B. JACKSON.

1. When the morning sun is bright, And the harvest fields are white, And the ones that should be reaping In the fields, are loit'ring by; When the Mas-ter's voice is ring-ing O'er the fields of wav-ing grain, Call-ing loud for reap-ers! an-swer, "Here am I, Here am I!"

2. There are famished souls to feed, There are wand'ring steps to lead; From the depths of sin and darkness, There are helpless ones that cry: "Who will feed the hun-gry chil-dren, Who will seek the lost to save?" Je-sus calls you, who will an-swer, "Here am I, Here am I!"

3. There are bat-tles yet to win, 'Gainst the marshalled host of sin, And the Sav-ior, in each con-flict Swift to help, is ev-er nigh; When He calls for deeds of dar-ing, And for loy-al hearts and true, Read-y will I be to an-swer, "Here am I, Here am I!"

D. S.—*ev - er Thou wilt have me do to glo - ri - fy Thy name,*
FINE.

Speak, O Lord, Thy servant hear-eth, Here am I, Here am I!"

CHORUS.
When I hear ...... the voice of my Sav - - ior,
When I hear the lov-ing voice, the lov-ing voice of my Sav-ior,

COPYRIGHT, 1897, BY CHAS. H. GABRIEL.

Here Am I.

No. 89. JUST ASK HIM IN TO STAY.

SILAS FARMER. CHAS. H. GABRIEL.

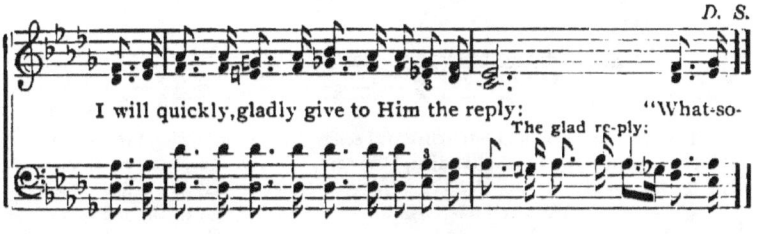

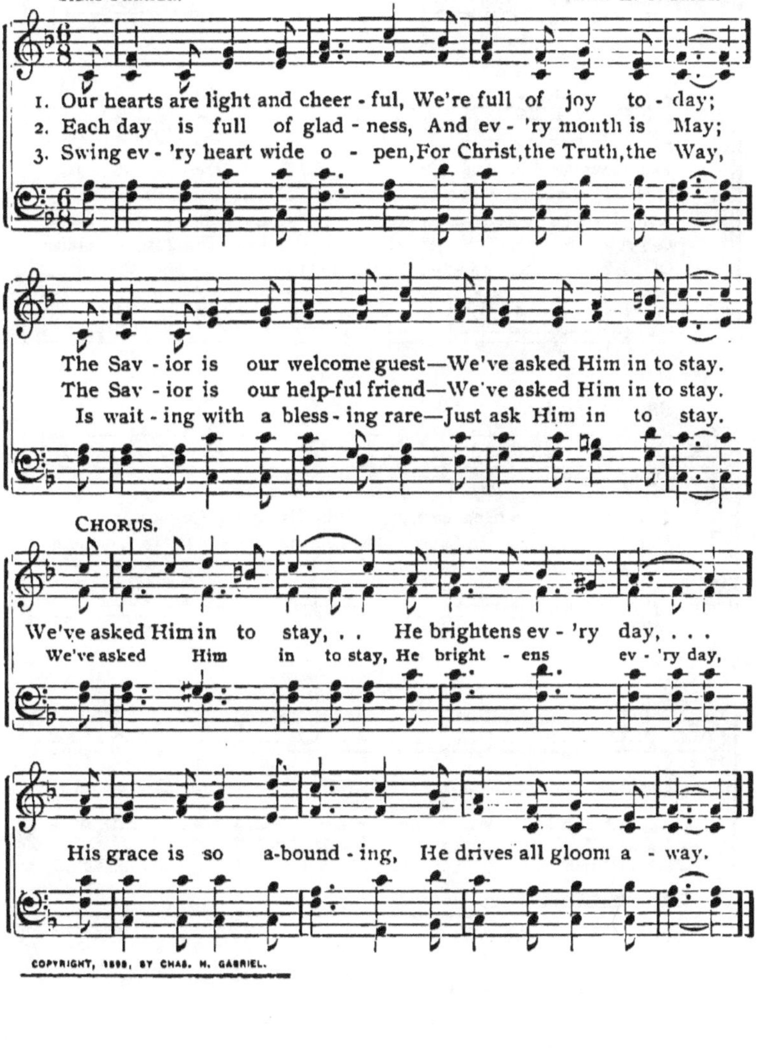

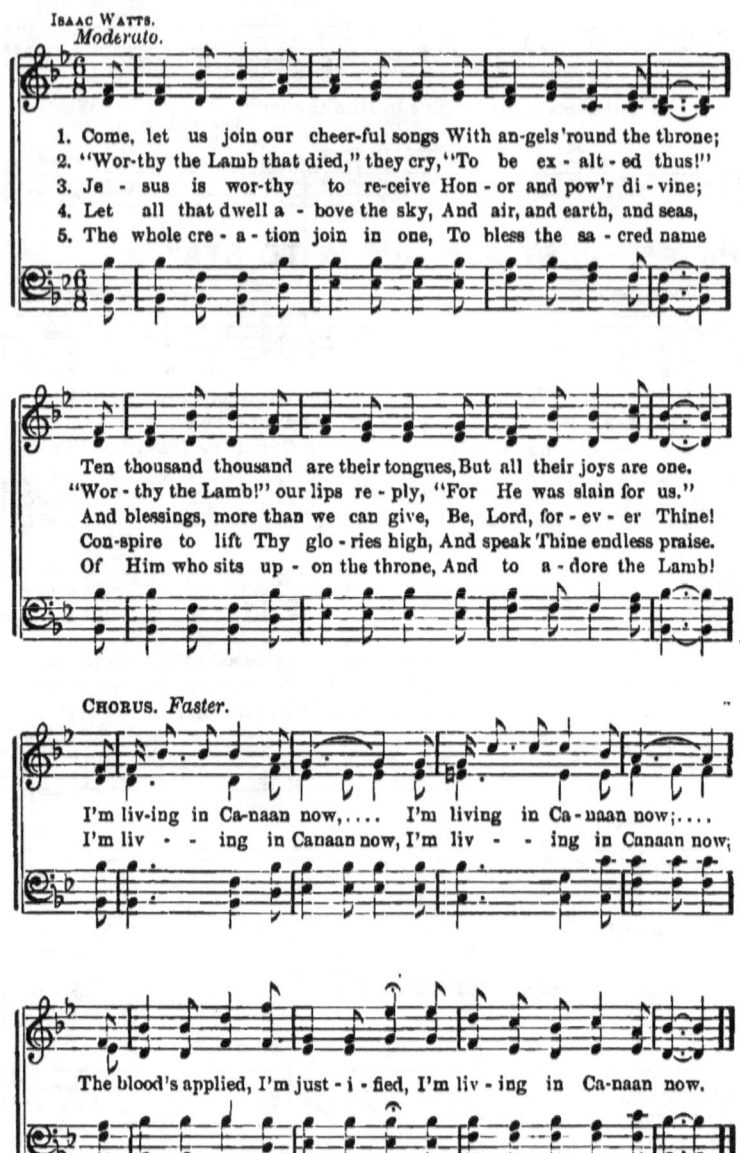

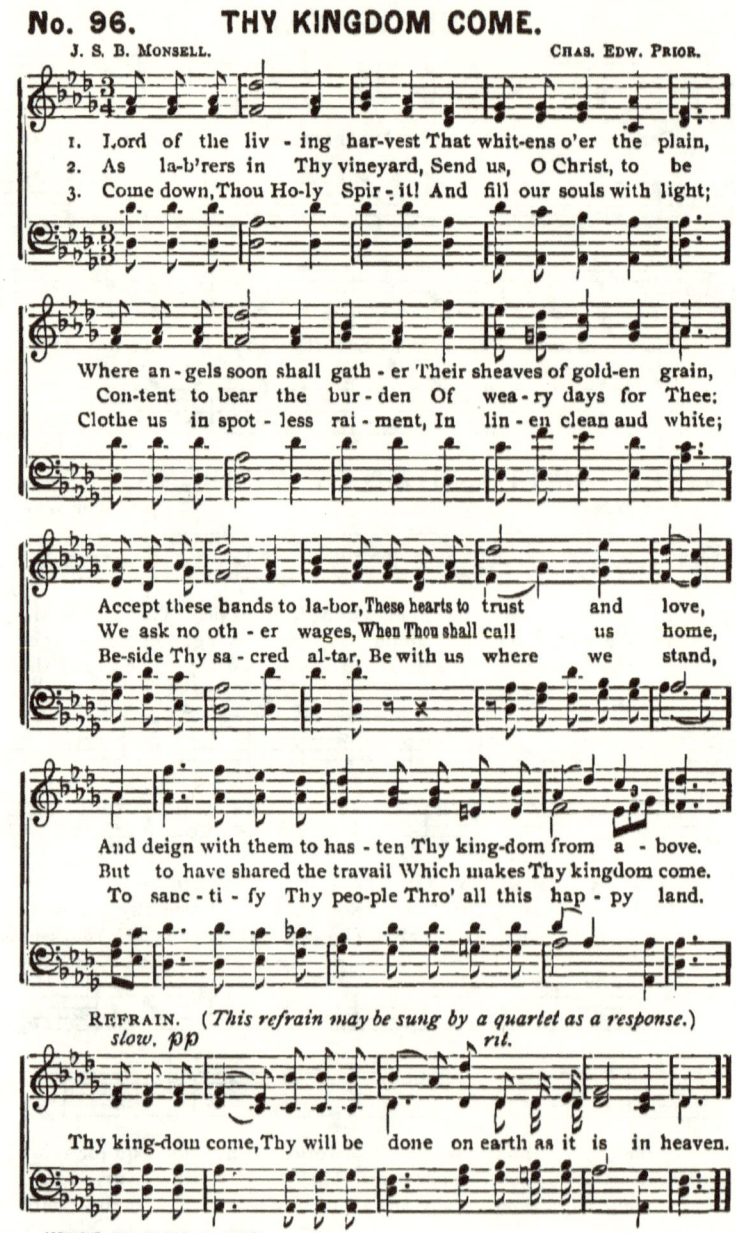

No. 99. THE MASTER COMES.

Rev. E. Gough. B. A. J. Newsome.

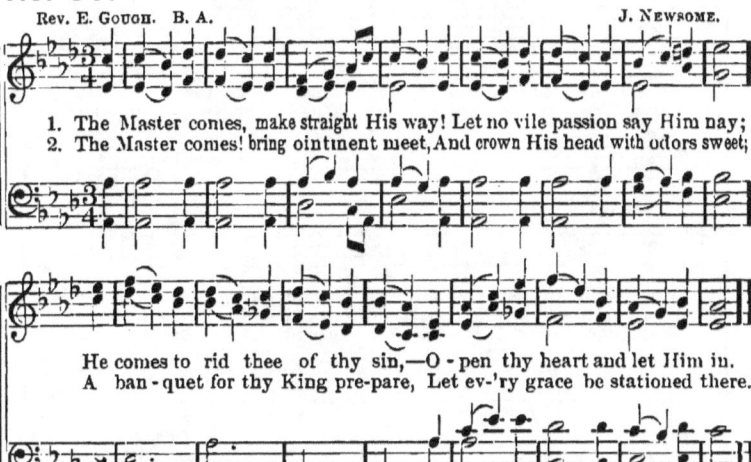

1. The Master comes, make straight His way! Let no vile passion say Him nay;
He comes to rid thee of thy sin,—O-pen thy heart and let Him in.
2. The Master comes! bring ointment meet, And crown His head with odors sweet;
A banquet for thy King prepare, Let ev-'ry grace be stationed there.

3
Give Peace her dove, give Praise her lyre,
Bid languid Love stir up her fire,
While Zeal stands ready to fulfill
Each counsel of the Savior's will.

4
The Master comes! search well Thy heart,
Bid Satan from the shrine depart;
Break down the idols prized so long,
Write a new coronation song.

5
The Master comes! O happy thou!
Before thy gates He standeth now;
From other works awhile forbear,—
To welcome Christ be all thy care.

6
The Master comes! His face we see;
O Jesus, we have longed for Thee;
Into our hearts Thy fulness bring,
And make us like Thee while we sing.

COPYRIGHT, 1894, BY CHAS. H. GABRIEL.

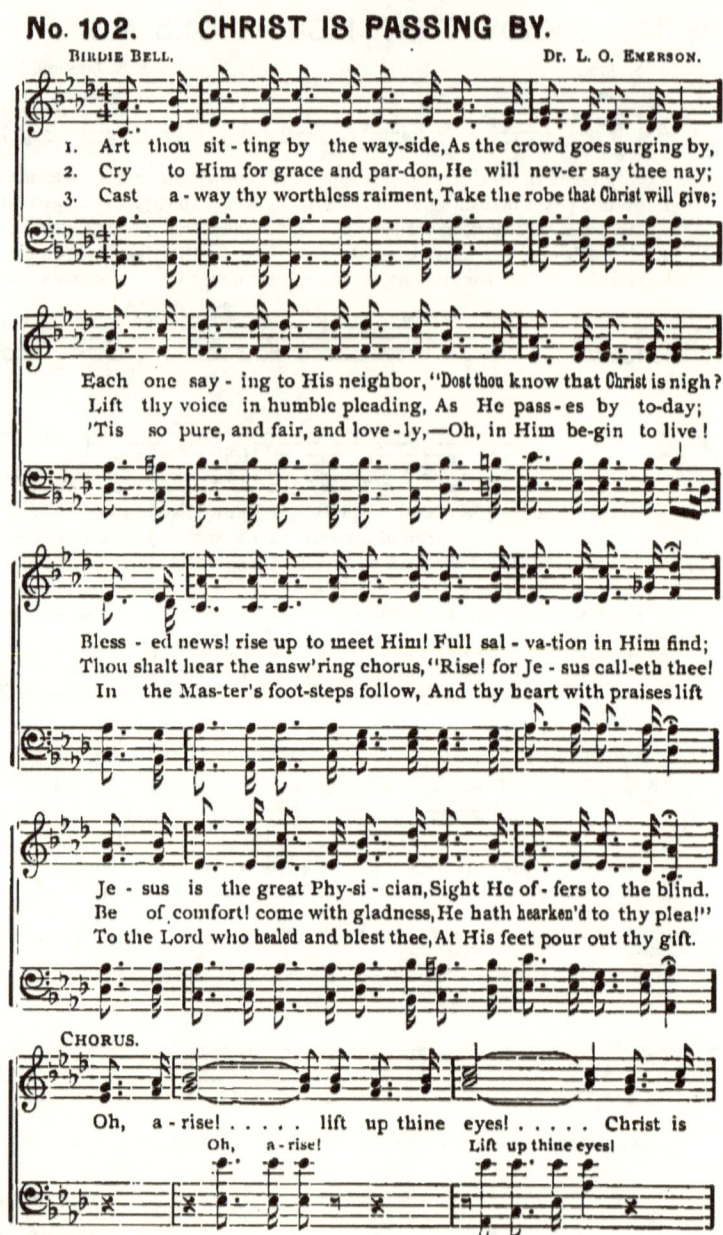

Christ is Passing By.

pass - - ing by to-day!....... He will heal...
Christ is pass-ing, pass-ing by to-day! He will heal
thee, He will save thee, Ere He pass - - es by to-day.
thee, He will save thee, Ere He pass-es by to-day.

No. 103. COME THOU, O TRAVELER.

J. E. RANKIN, D. D.   CHAS. H. GABRIEL.

1. Come thou, O trav-'ler blest, Seek-ing to be a guest
2. Spread thou the Pas-chal feast; From E-gypt's bonds re-leased,
3. Tem-ple, hence-forth, of Thine, Mark'd by Thy lin-tel sign,

With-in my soul; My heart, oppressed and sore, Throws o-pen
Come, sup with me; On Thee I lean my head, Break Thou the
Sprin-kled with blood; Loins gird-ed now I stand. Faith's staff with-

wide the door; Welcome for-ev-er-more: Take full con-trol.
liv-ing bread, Pour Thou the wine once shed On Cal-va-ry.
in my hand, To cross to Canaan's land, Death's an-gry flood.

COPYRIGHT, 1894, BY CHAS. H. GABRIEL.

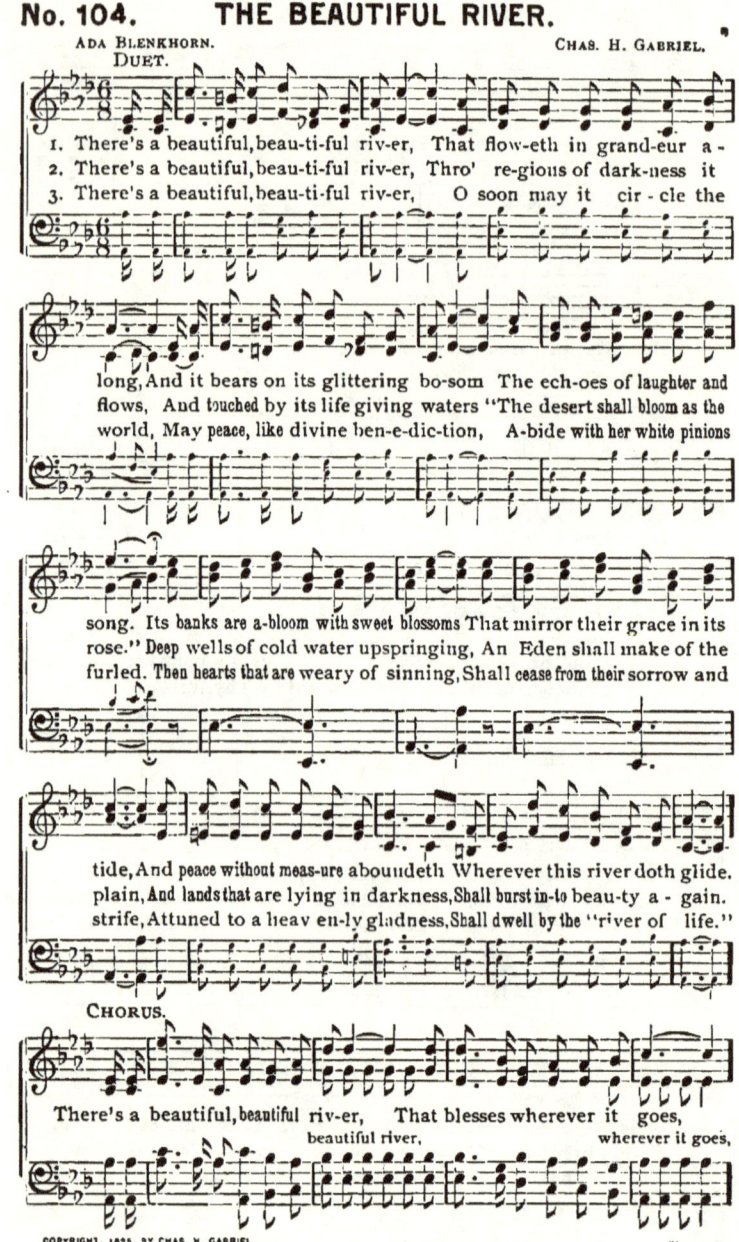

The Beautiful River.

This beautiful, beautiful riv-er. From the City of God it flows.
beau-ti-ful riv-er, it flows.

No. 105. THE REAPER MAY CALL TO-NIGHT.

MAGGIE E. GREGORY. H. A. HENRY.

1. The reaper may call for you to-night; Oh, are you ready, my brother?
2. The Savior now waits your soul to bless, Brother, why will you so grieve Him?
3. The Spirit yet strives, and pleads, and waits; Will you not hear Him, my brother?

To-day is yours! then use it a-right, You nev-er may see an-oth-er.
Oh, hasten now your sins to con-fess And open your heart, re-ceive Him.
To-day is yours; come, ere you're too late, You nev-er may see an-oth-er.

CHORUS.

The reaper may call for you to-night; Have you a ti-tle to mansions of light?

The Sav-ior is pleading, oh, why will you slight; He's pleading to-night, my broth-er.

COPYRIGHT, 1895, BY CHAS. H. GABRIEL.

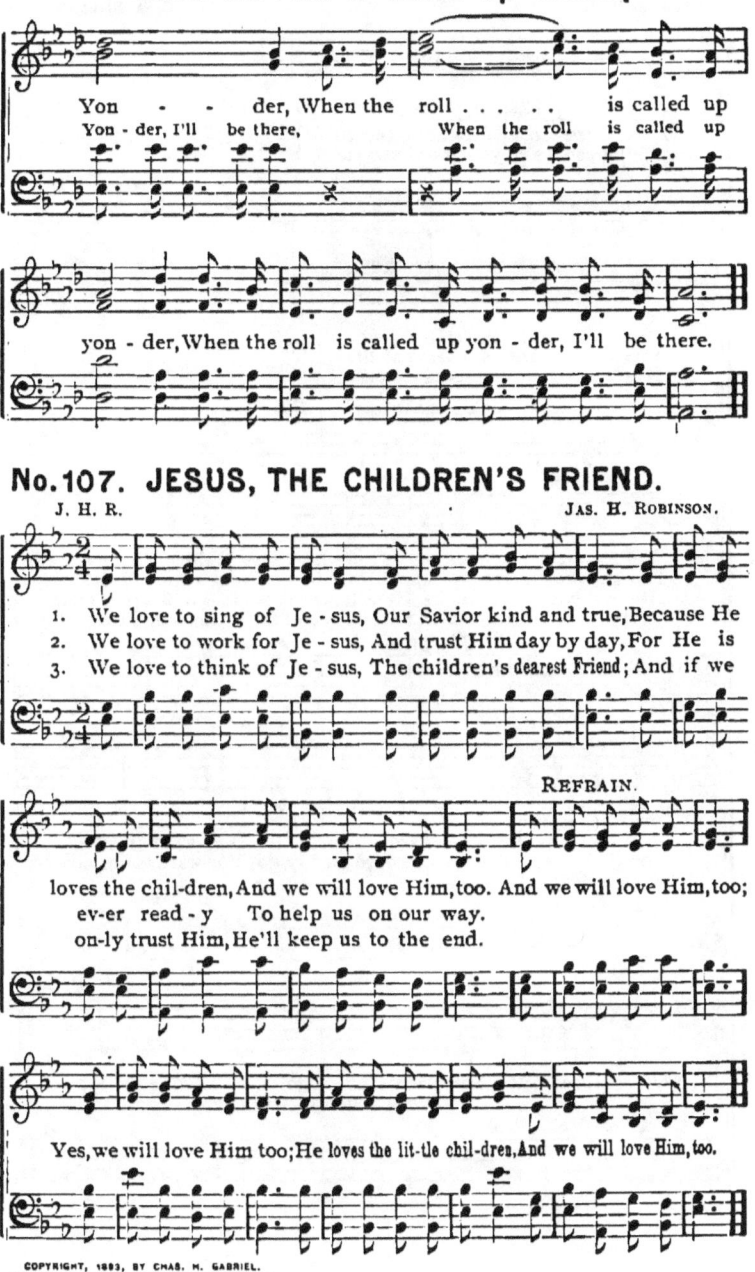

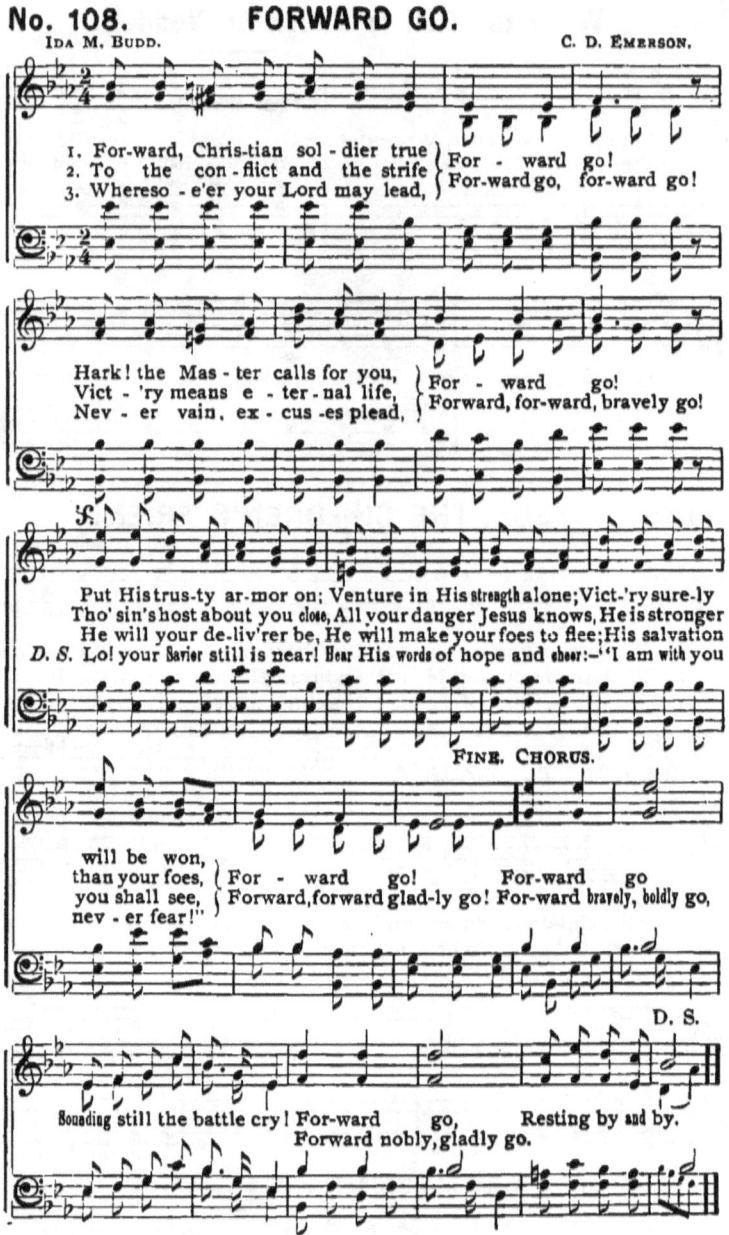

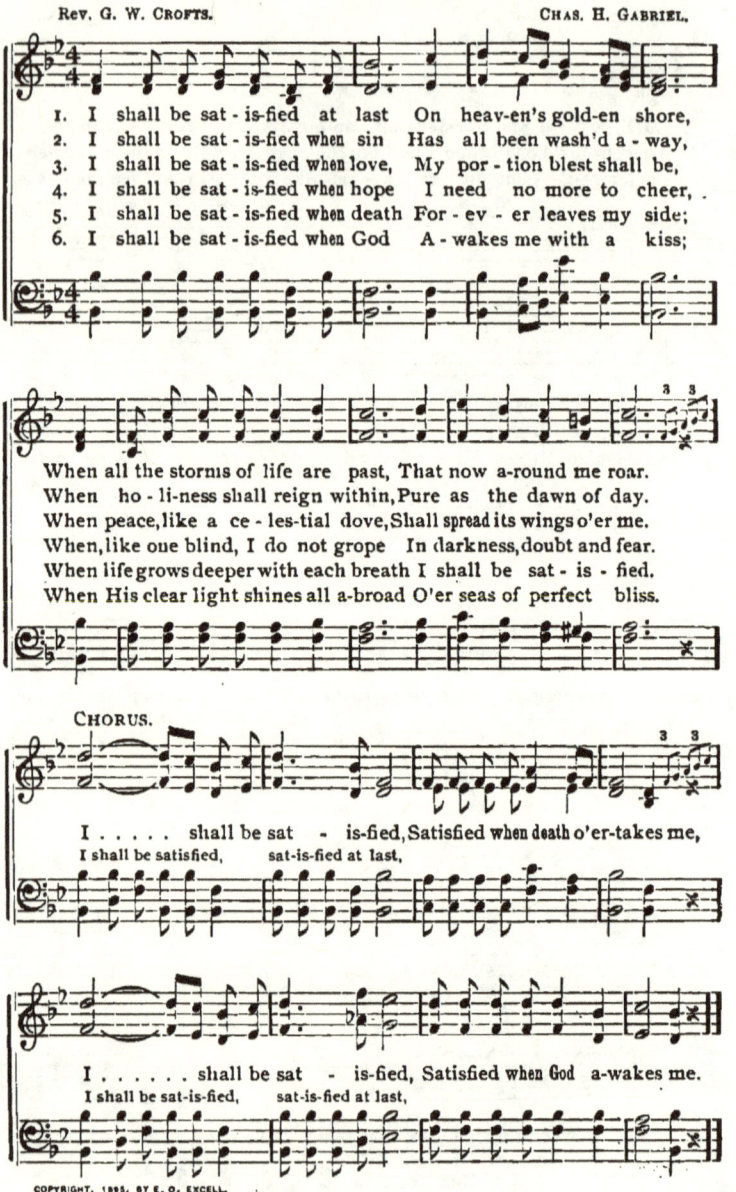

No. 113. SAFE WITH THEE.

ETTA HARBOUR.   H. A. HENRY.

1. Safe with Thee, O ten-der Shepherd, Lead me gent-ly day by day;
2. 'Twas Thy love that sought and found me. Kindest Shepherd ever known,
3. Safe with Thee, O ten-der Shepherd, Now up-on Thy staff I lean.

In Thy pleasant pastures feed me, Keep my soul, O Lord, I pray.
For Thy sheep from Thee had wandered, And was fainting and a-lone.
It supports and gives me comfort, And Thy blood it makes me clean.

CHORUS.

O, pa-tient, ten-der Shep-herd Blest Guard-ian of thy sheep,

No more from Thee I'll wan-der, But near Thy side I'll keep.

COPYRIGHT, 1897, BY CHAS. H. GABRIEL.

Source of Every Blessing.

Thou art the light of life to me;
Thou art the light.......... of life to me;..........

All my sins.......... to Thee con-fess - - ing,
yea, all my sins to Thee con-fess-ing,

Rit.

Yea, Thou wilt cleanse and par-don me..........
Thou wilt cleanse.......... and par-don me, and pardon me.

No. 115. DEPTH OF MERCY.

CHARLES WESLEY.   J. STEVENSON.

1. { Depth of mer-cy, can there be Mer-cy still re-served for me?
    Can my God His wrath for-bear, Me, the chief of sin-ners, spare? }
2. { I have long withstood His grace; Long provoked Him to His face;
    Would not harken to His calls; Grieved Him by a thousand falls. }
3. { Now in-cline me to re-lent; Let me now my sins la-ment;
    Now my foul re-volt de-plore, Weep, be-lieve, and sin no more. }

REFRAIN.

{ God is love, I know, I feel;
  Jesus weeps and loves me still; } Je-sus weeps, He weeps and loves me still.

The Ark of His Love.

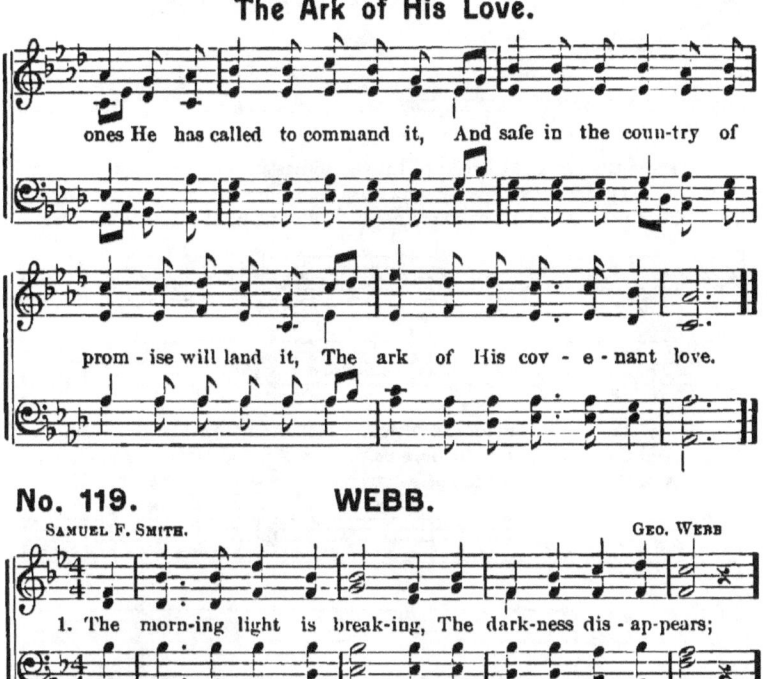

...ones He has called to command it, And safe in the country of promise will land it, The ark of His covenant love.

No. 119.   WEBB.

SAMUEL F. SMITH.   GEO. WEBB.

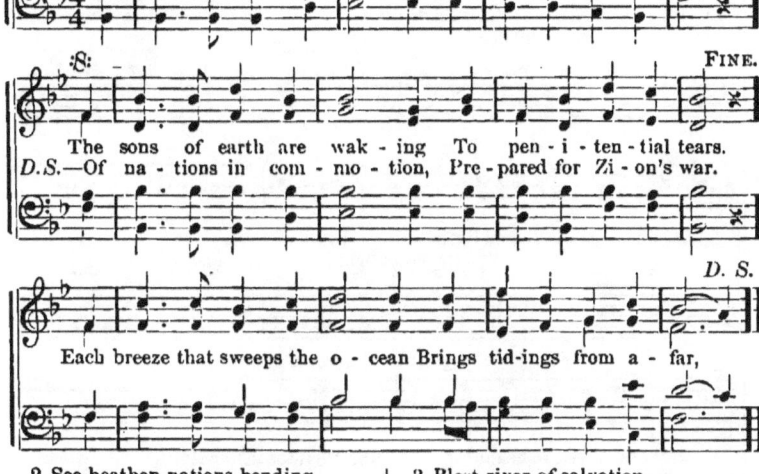

1. The morning light is breaking, The darkness disappears;
The sons of earth are waking To penitential tears.
D.S.—Of nations in commotion, Prepared for Zion's war.

Each breeze that sweeps the ocean Brings tidings from afar,

2 See heathen nations bending
   Before the God we love,
And thousand hearts ascending
   In gratitude above;
While sinners, now confessing
   The gospel call, obey,
And seek the Savior's blessing,
   A nation in a day.

3 Blest river of salvation,
   Pursue thine onward way;
Flow thou to every nation,
   Nor in thy richness stay:
Stay not till all the lowly
   Triumphant reach their home:
Stay not till all the holy
   Proclaim, "The Lord is come!"

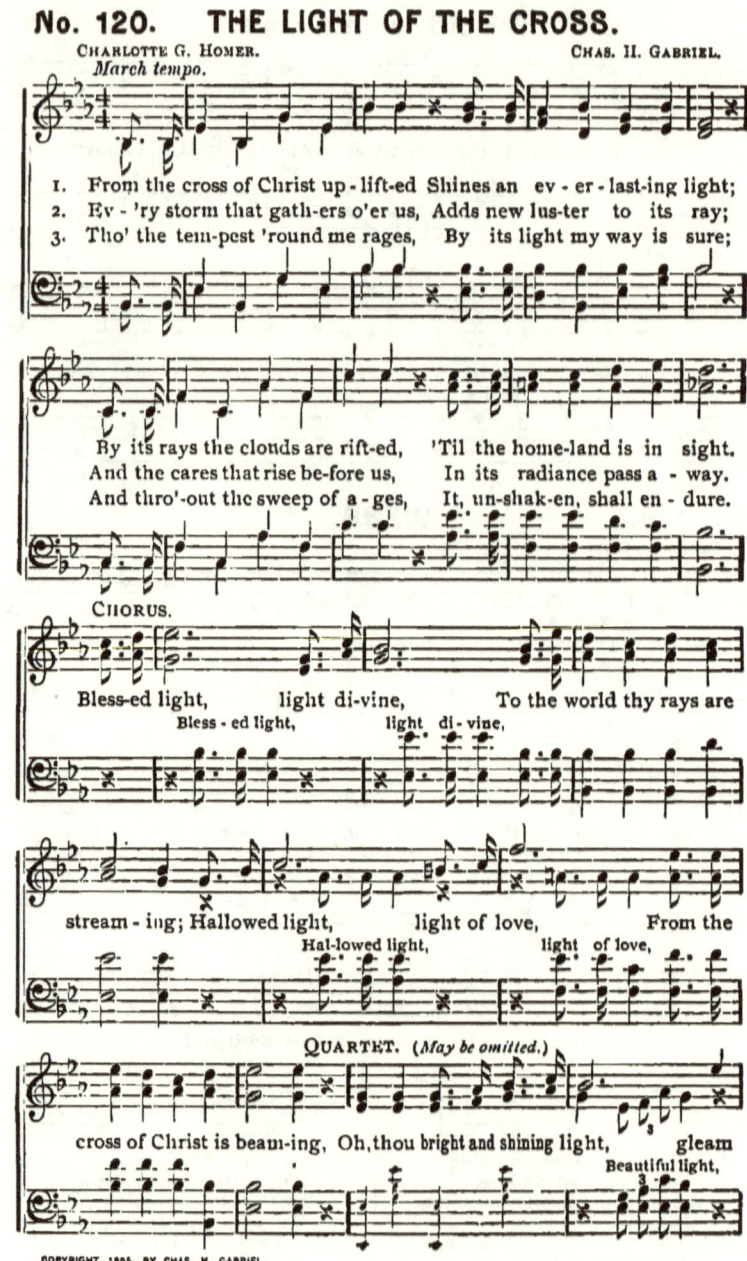

Can it Be?

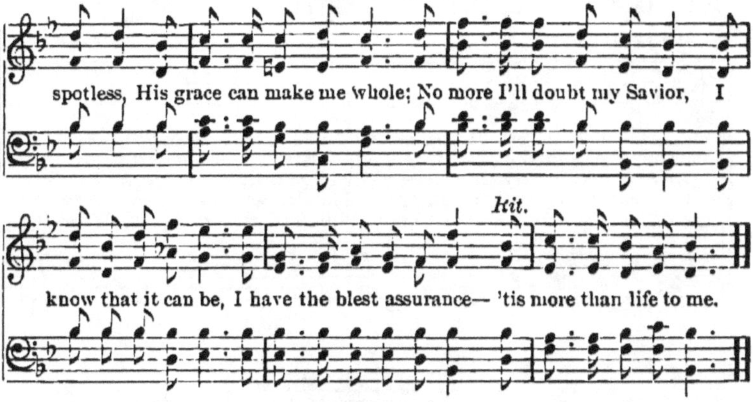

spotless, His grace can make me whole; No more I'll doubt my Savior, I know that it can be, I have the blest assurance— 'tis more than life to me.

No. 123. WHEN THE MIGHTY TRUMP.

ISAAC NAYLOR.

1. { The thun-ders of judg-ment shall crash through the skies,
     The dead, small and great, from their graves shall a-rise. }
2. { The cry shall be heard that the Bride-groom hath come
     To take His blest Bride to His own sa-cred home. }
3. { On the morn-ing of judg-ment, oh, where will you stand?
     On the left of the Shepherd, or at His right hand? }
4. { The lost one, in an-guish and sor-row and dread,
     Shall call for the mountains to fall on his head! }

ff CHORUS.

When the might-y, might-y, might-y trump Sounds, "Come, come a-way!" Oh, may we be read-y To hail that great day.

COPYRIGHT, 1894, BY CHAS. H. GABRIEL.

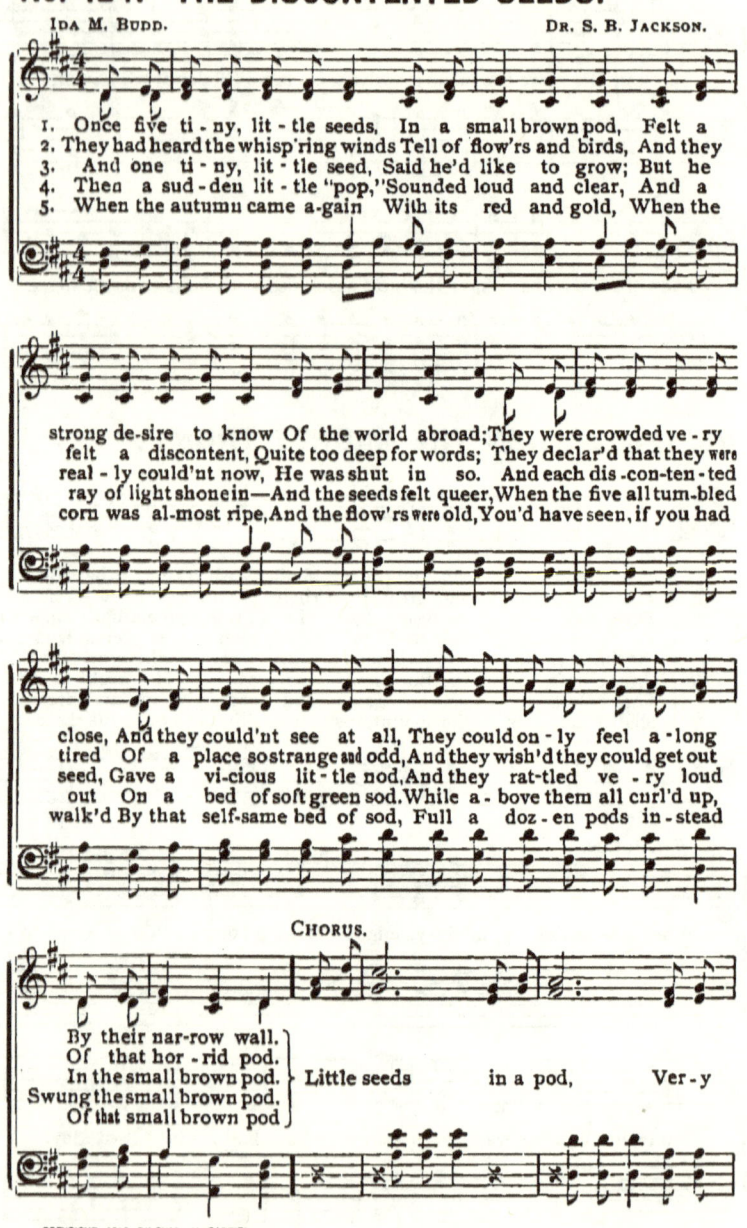

God's Mansions are Open.

list! 'tis a voice! "Come and follow me; God's mansions are o-pen to thee."
list to the voice! "Come and follow me; God's mansions are o-pen to thee."
ech-o the call! "Come and follow me; God's mansions are o-pen to thee."

CHORUS.

God's mansions are o-pen to thee to-night, God's mansions are open to thee; (to thee;) There's

Rit.

death on the mountain of sin to-night, But God's mansions are open to thee.

No. 127. THE LORD'S PRAYER. No. 2.

1. Our Father, which art in heaven, | Hallowed | be Thy | name.‖
   Thy kingdom come. Thy will be done on earth, as it | is in | heaven.
2. Give us this | day our daily | bread.‖
   And forgive us our debts, as | we for - | give our | debtors.
3. And lead us not into temptation, but de - | liver | us from evil:‖
   For Thine is the kingdom, and the power, and the glory,
   for - | ever, and | ever, A - | men.

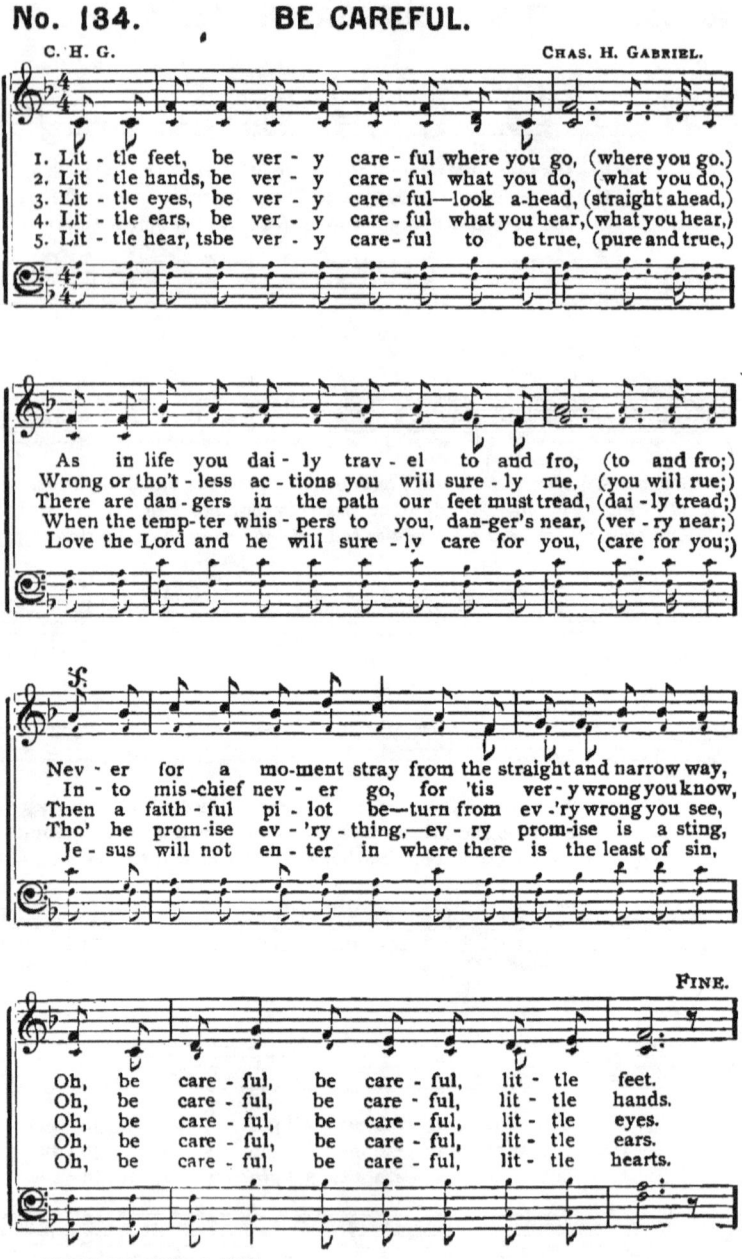

Be Careful.

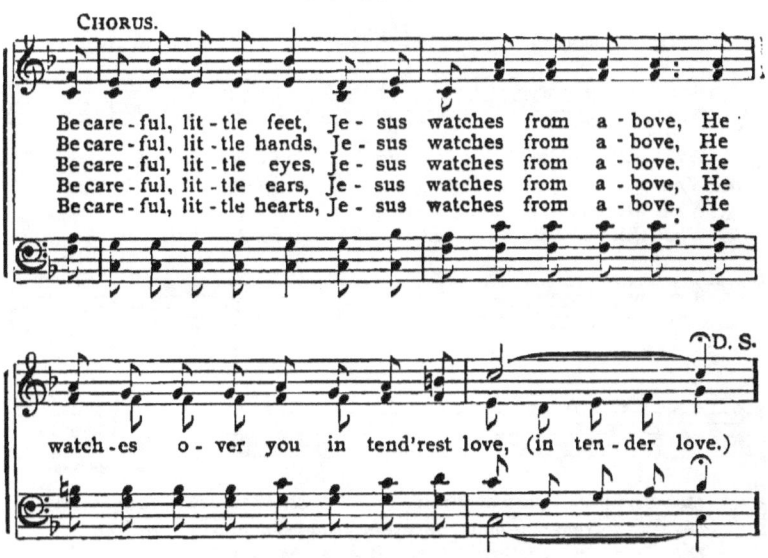

No. 135. THE LIFE, THE TRUTH, THE WAY.

IDA M. BUDD.   DR. S. B. JACKSON.

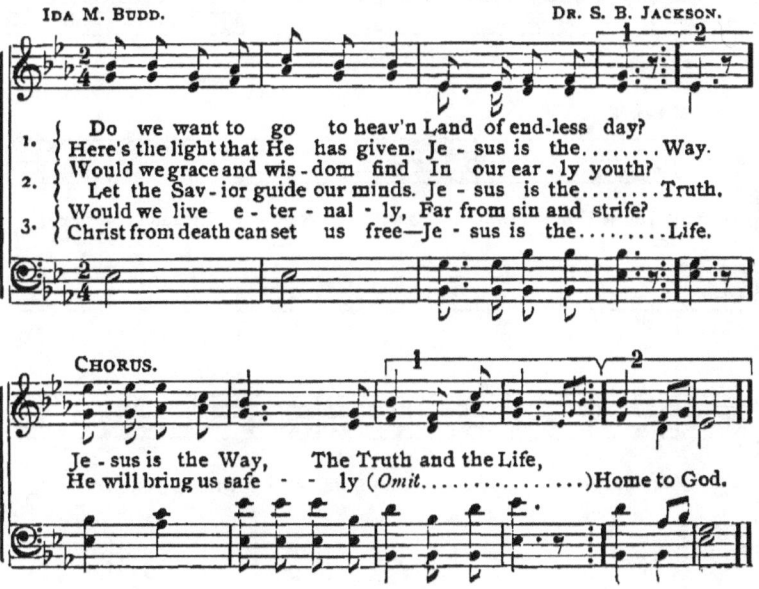

No. 137. MORE LOVE TO THEE.

MAGGIE E. GREGORY. H. A. HENRY.

1. Near-er to Thee, my Sav-ior, My long-ing heart would be;
2. O may Thy lov-ing kind-ness Sub-due my self-ish will,
3. Near-er to Thee,—still near-er, Dear Sav-ior, I would be;

Grant me Thy lov-ing fa-vor, Oh, draw me near-er Thee.
Re-move my car-nal blind-ness, And with Thy spir-it fill;
Thy love is sweet-er, dear-er, Than earth-ly joy to me;

I know that full and bound-less Thy love is un-to me, While
O melt my stub-born na-ture, I ask it o'er and o'er; With
Grant me to feel thy pres-ence, Thy smil-ing face to see, And,

Fine.

mine is oft-en faint and cold,—Give me more love to Thee!
all Thy bless-ed full-ness fill, And help me love Thee more.
gra-cious Lord, bap-tize my heart With more of love to Thee!

D. S.—*This my pray'r shall ev-er be, More love, more love to Thee.*

CHORUS. *D. S.*

More love to Thee, More love to Thee,
to Thee, to Thee,

COPYRIGHT, 1898, BY CHAS. H. GABRIEL.

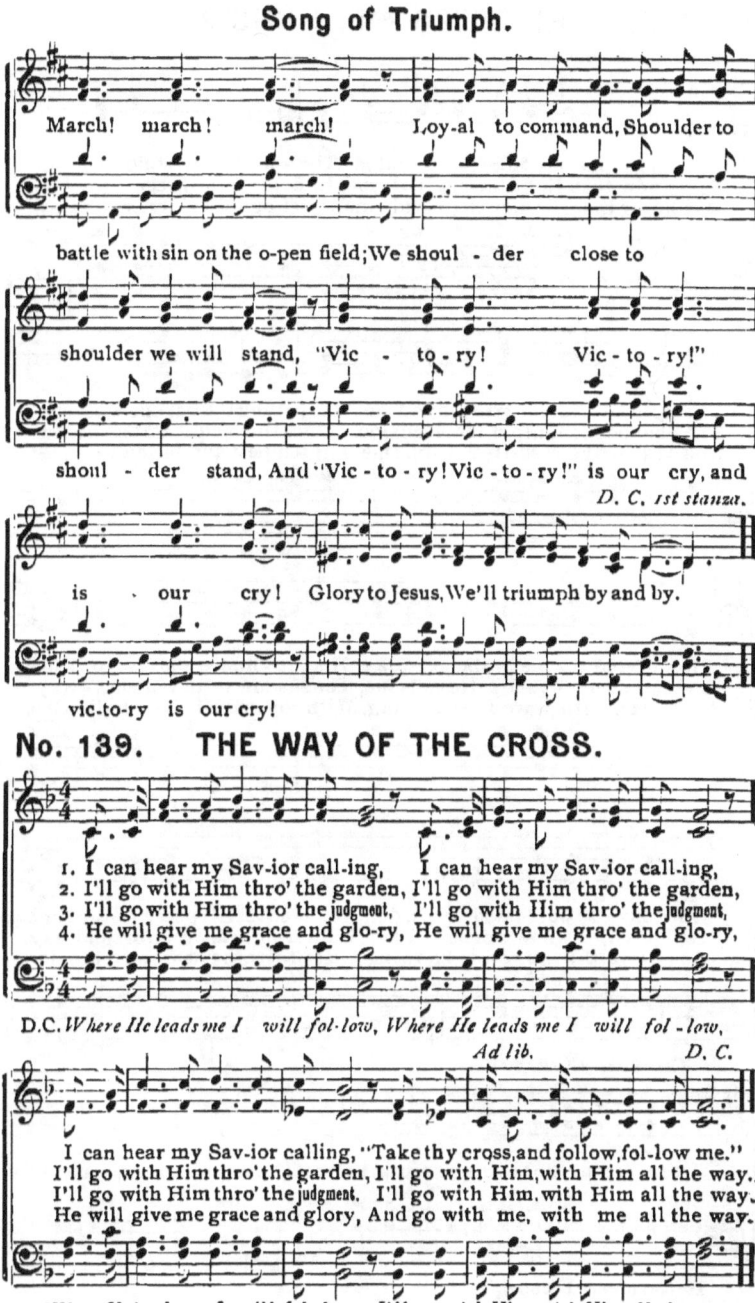

He Saves Me, I Know.

cleanses e-ven me. The blood that washes white as snow Now cleanses e-ven me.

No. 141. TELL IT ALL TO JESUS.

WILLIAM H. GARDNER.   CHAS. H. GABRIEL.

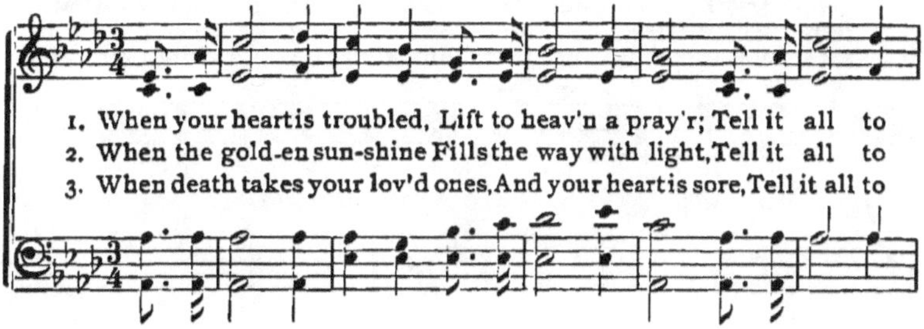

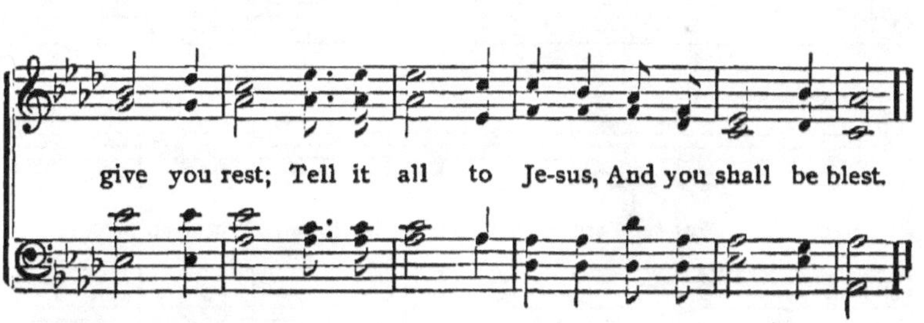

1. When your heart is troubled, Lift to heav'n a pray'r; Tell it all to
2. When the gold-en sun-shine Fills the way with light, Tell it all to
3. When death takes your lov'd ones, And your heart is sore, Tell it all to

REFRAIN.

Je - sus, He is list-'ning there.
Je - sus, All your joys re - cite. } Tell it all to Je - sus, He will
Jesus, He'll give peace once more.

give you rest; Tell it all to Je-sus, And you shall be blest.

COPYRIGHT, 1899, BY CHAS. H. GABRIEL.

Beautiful Raiment.

wondrous beau-ty, Bought with His precious blood on Cal - va - ry.

No. 145. SWEET NAME OF JESUS.

Rev. W. C. Martin.   B. C. Unseld.

1. There is a name I love to hear, so sweet, so sweet;
2. When-e'er I hear the Sav-ior's name so sweet, so sweet,
3. His name I whis-per o'er and o'er so sweet, so sweet,

With mel - o - dy and gen-tle cheer re - plete, re-plete.
It helps to make love's ten - der flame com - plete, com-plete.
Who waits my soul on yon-der shore to greet, to greet.

Refrain.

O name of gen - tle maj - es - ty; O name of more than life to me;

How oft-en over I repeat: "Je-sus," "Jesus," always sweet, so sweet.

COPYRIGHT, 1898, BY E. S. LORENZ.

Zion Triumphant.

hap-pi-est meas-ure, Prais-es to Je-sus, our glo-ri-fied King.

No. 147. GENTLY LEAD US.

THOMAS HASTINGS.

1. Gently, Lord, oh, gen-tly lead us, Pilgrims in this vale of tears,
2. In the hour of pain and an-guish, In the hour when death draws near,

Thro' the tri-als yet de-creed us, Till our last great change ap-pears.
Suf-fer not our hearts to lan-guish, Suf-fer not our souls to fear;

When temptation's darts as-sail us, When in devious paths we stray,
And, when mor-tal life is end-ed, Bid us in Thine arms to rest,

Let Thy good-ness nev-er fail us, Lead us in Thy per-fect way.
Till, by an-gel hands at-tend-ed, We a-wake a-mong the blest.

No. 151. LITTLE PILGRIMS.

IDA M. BUDD. DR. S. B. JACKSON.

1. We are lit-tle pil-grims, Walk-ing in the light, Bear-ing ti-ny cross-es, Wear-ing garments white. In the nar-row way, Going home to heaven, And e-ter-nal day.
2. Keeping close to Je-sus, Trust-ing in His care, All our lit-tle cross-es, He will help us bear. Spotless, pure and clean, He will make us ever Free from guilt and sin.
3. Keeping close to je-sus, Some day by and by We shall find a conn-try Far be-yond the sky. Of that land so fair, We shall dwell forever, Safe with Jesus there.

Keep-ing close to Je-sus, He will keep our white robes And in some bright mansion

D. S.—Keeping close to Jesus, Walking in the light.

CHORUS.

We are lit-tle pilgrims, March, march, march! Keeping close to Jesus.

March, march, march, We are little pilgrims robed in garments white,

COPYRIGHT, 1897, BY CHAS. H. GABRIEL.

Jesus is Calling.

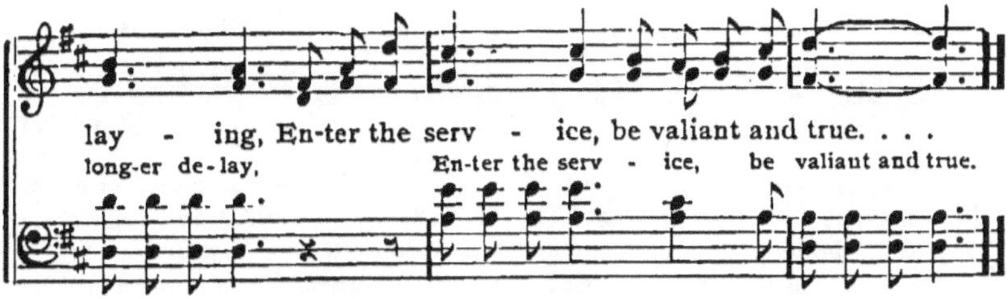

lay - ing, En-ter the serv - ice, be valiant and true....
long-er de-lay, En-ter the serv - ice, be valiant and true.

No. 155. CAN YOU DOUBT HIM?

FRED WOODROW.   Dr. W. H. DOANE.

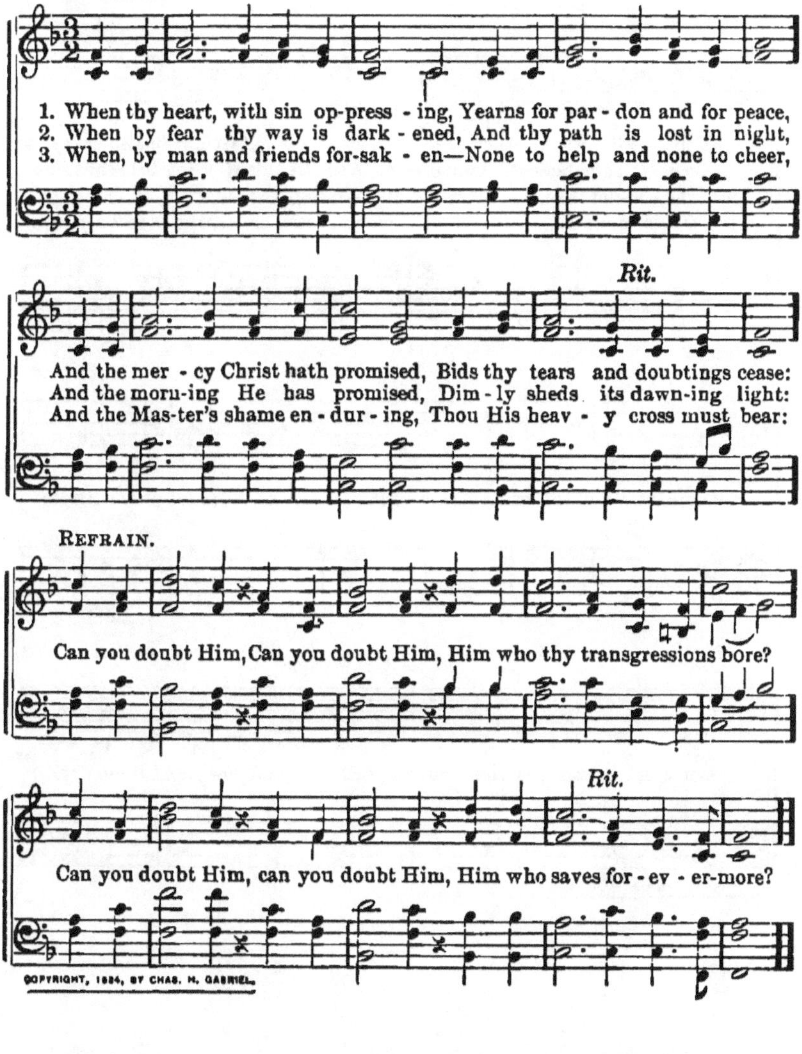

1. When thy heart, with sin op-press - ing, Yearns for par - don and for peace,
2. When by fear thy way is dark - ened, And thy path is lost in night,
3. When, by man and friends for-sak - en—None to help and none to cheer,

And the mer - cy Christ hath promised, Bids thy tears and doubtings cease:
And the morn-ing He has promised, Dim - ly sheds its dawn-ing light:
And the Mas-ter's shame en - dur - ing, Thou His heav - y cross must bear:

REFRAIN.

Can you doubt Him, Can you doubt Him, Him who thy transgressions bore?

Can you doubt Him, can you doubt Him, Him who saves for - ev - er-more?

COPYRIGHT, 1884, BY CHAS. H. GABRIEL.

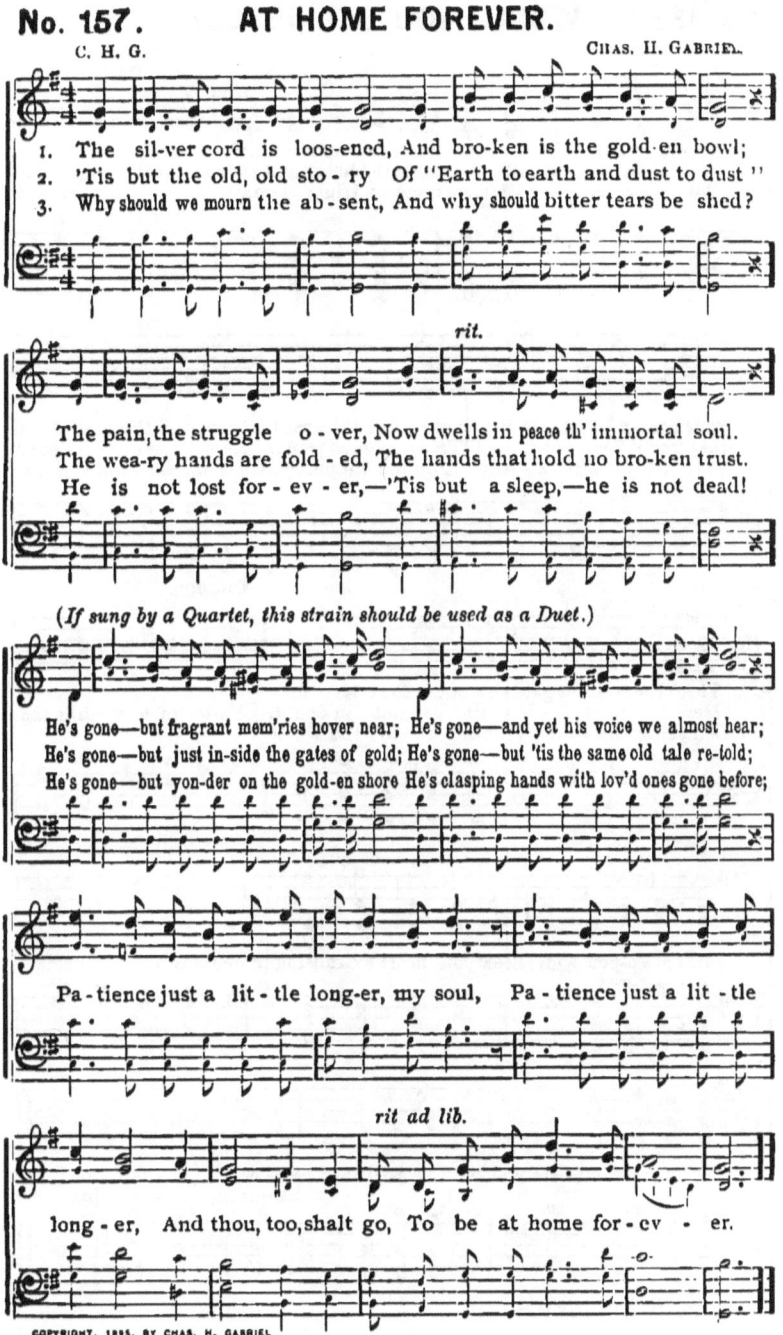

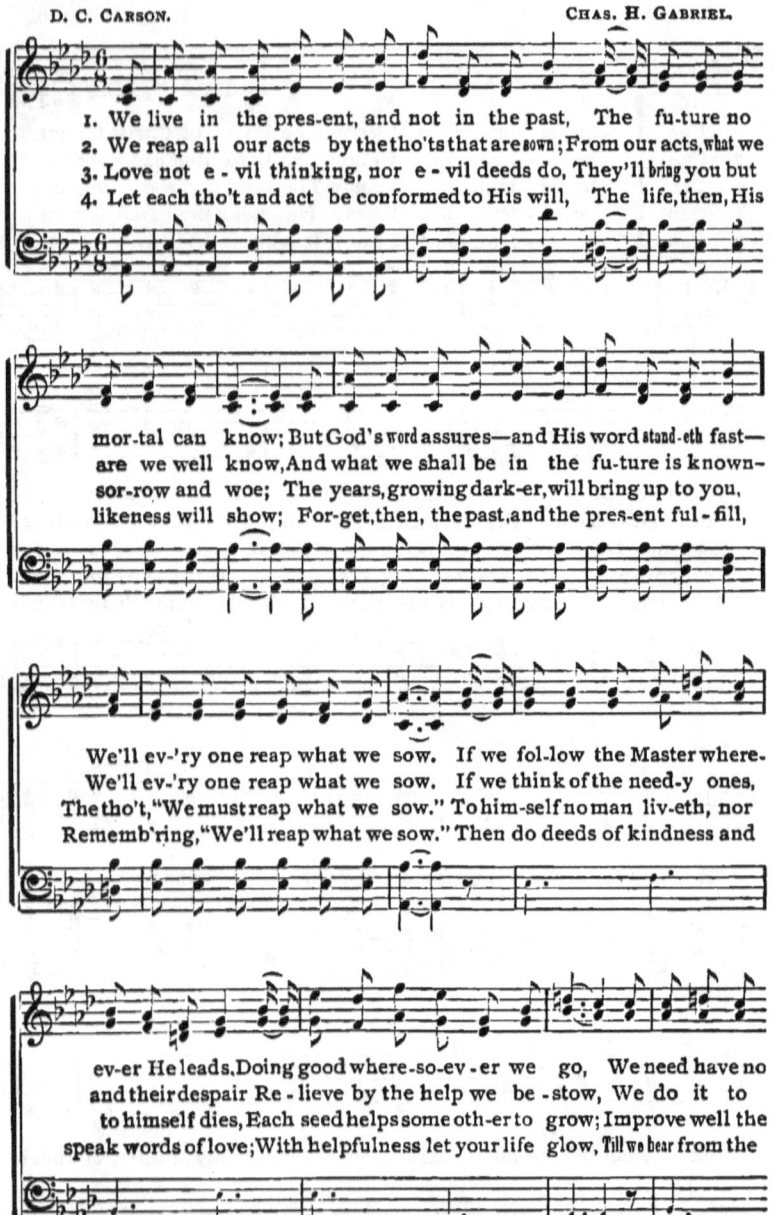

Conquering Grace.

love and joy we sing While toil-ing ev-er toil-ing on......
toil..........ing on, toiling on.

No. 163. I CAN ALWAYS TRUST HIM.

WM. H. GARDNER.   CHAS. H. GABRIEL.

1. I can al-ways trust Him, He is ev-er near;
2. I can al-ways trust Him, And I say each day—
3. I can al-ways trust Him, For His word is sure;

Pa-tient-ly He's wait-ing, All my pray'rs to hear.
With my lov-ing Sav-ior, Hap-py is the way."
And thro' count-less a-ges It will thus en-dure.

CHORUS.

I can al-ways trust Him, Trust Him, come what may;......
I can al-ways trust Him, Trust Him, come what may;

Bless-ed, bless-ed Je-sus, Lead me day by day!
Bless-ed, bless-ed Je-sus,

COPYRIGHT, 1898, BY CHAS. H. GABRIEL.

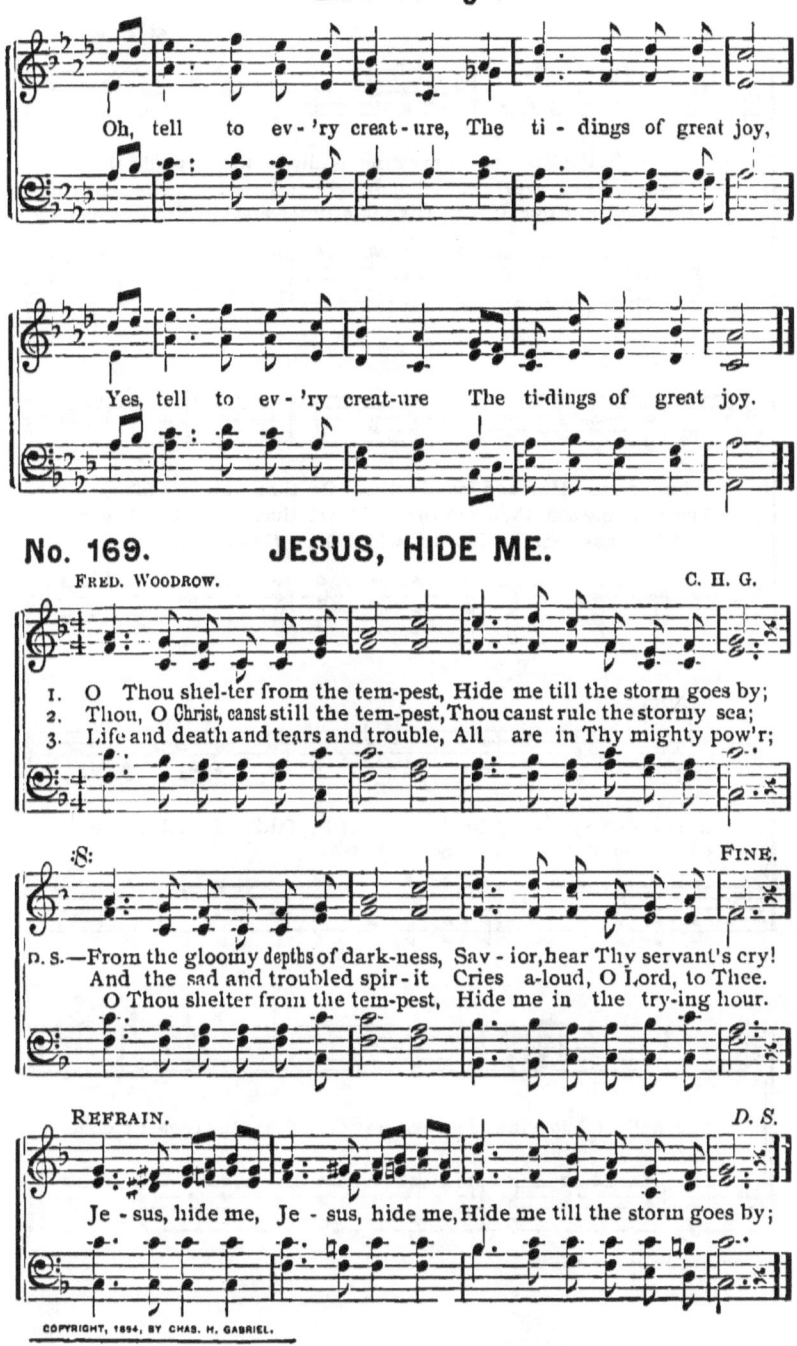

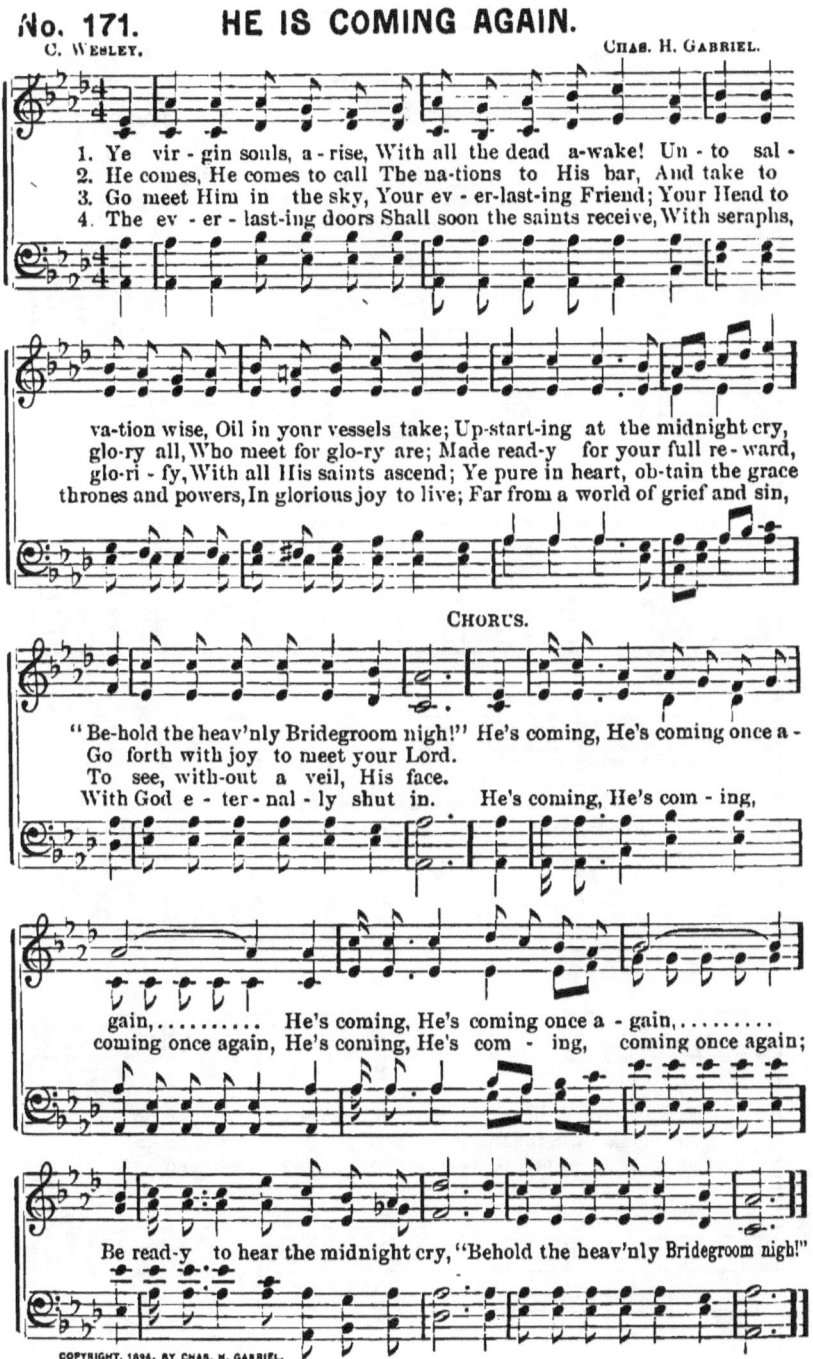

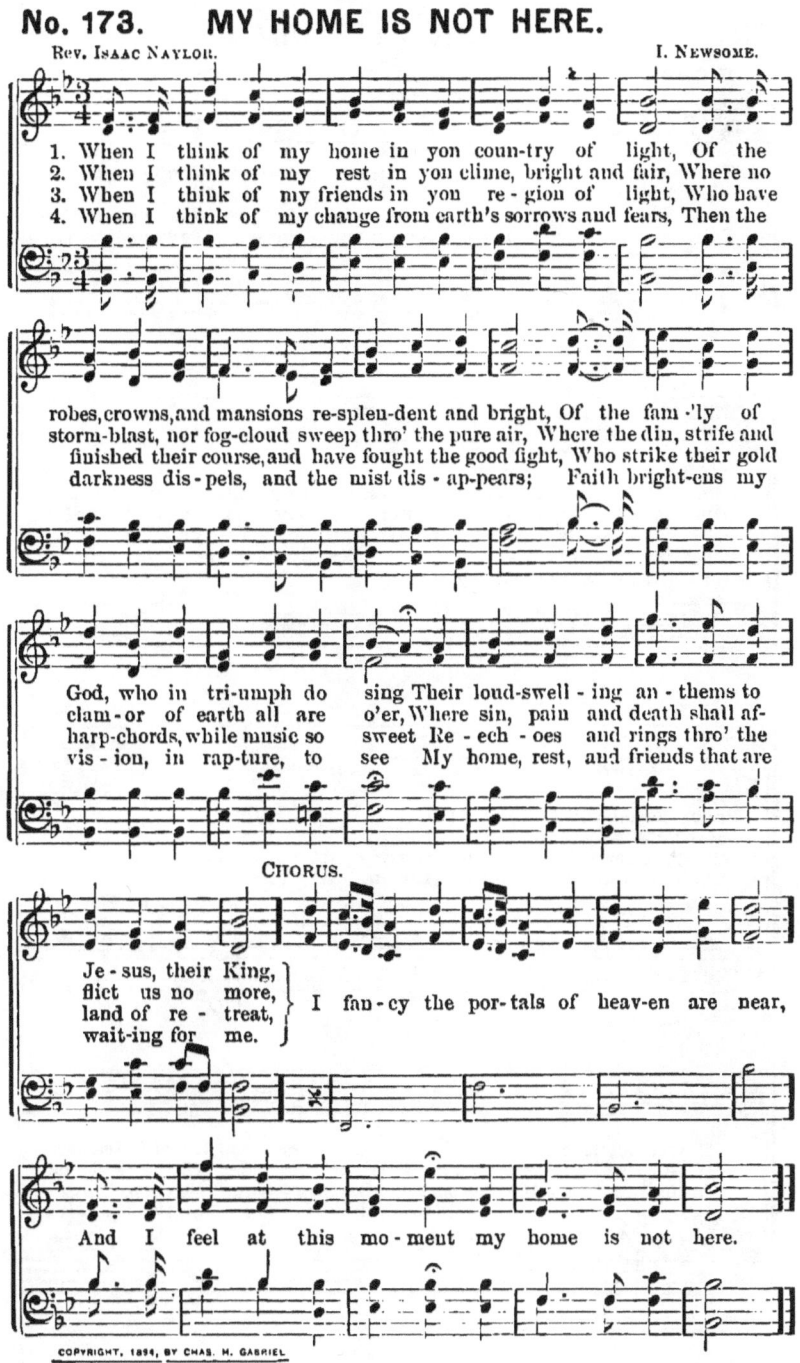

No. 175.   DENNIS.

1 Blest be the tie that binds
   Our hearts in christian love;
   The fellowship of kindred minds
   Is like to that above.

2 Before our Father's throne,
   We pour our ardent prayers;
   Our hopes, our fears, our aims are one,
   Our comforts and our cares.

3 We share our mutual woes,
   Our mutual burdens bear;
   And often for each other flows
   The sympathizing tear.

4 When we asunder part,
   It gives us inward pain;
   But we shall still be joined in heart,
   And hope to meet again.

No. 177. SING JOYFULLY, SING CHEERILY.

ADA BLENKHORN. H. A. HENRY.

1. When skies are blue a-bove our head And sunshine gilds the day,—
2. When storm-clouds gath-er on our sight, Rude winds a-bout us blow,
3. Should no kind friend a hand ex-tend To help us when we fall,—

When fra-grant flow'rs a-dorn our path In fair and bright a-ray:—
The sharp thorns pierce our feet and hands Which-ev-er way we go:—
Strength to the heart this tho't af-fords—Our God is o-ver all:—

CHORUS.

Sing hope-ful-ly, Sing cheer-i-ly, All a-long the line,
sing   sing

And let our songs with joy resound,—The glo-ry, Lord, be Thine.

COPYRIGHT, 1895, BY CHAS. H. GABRIEL.

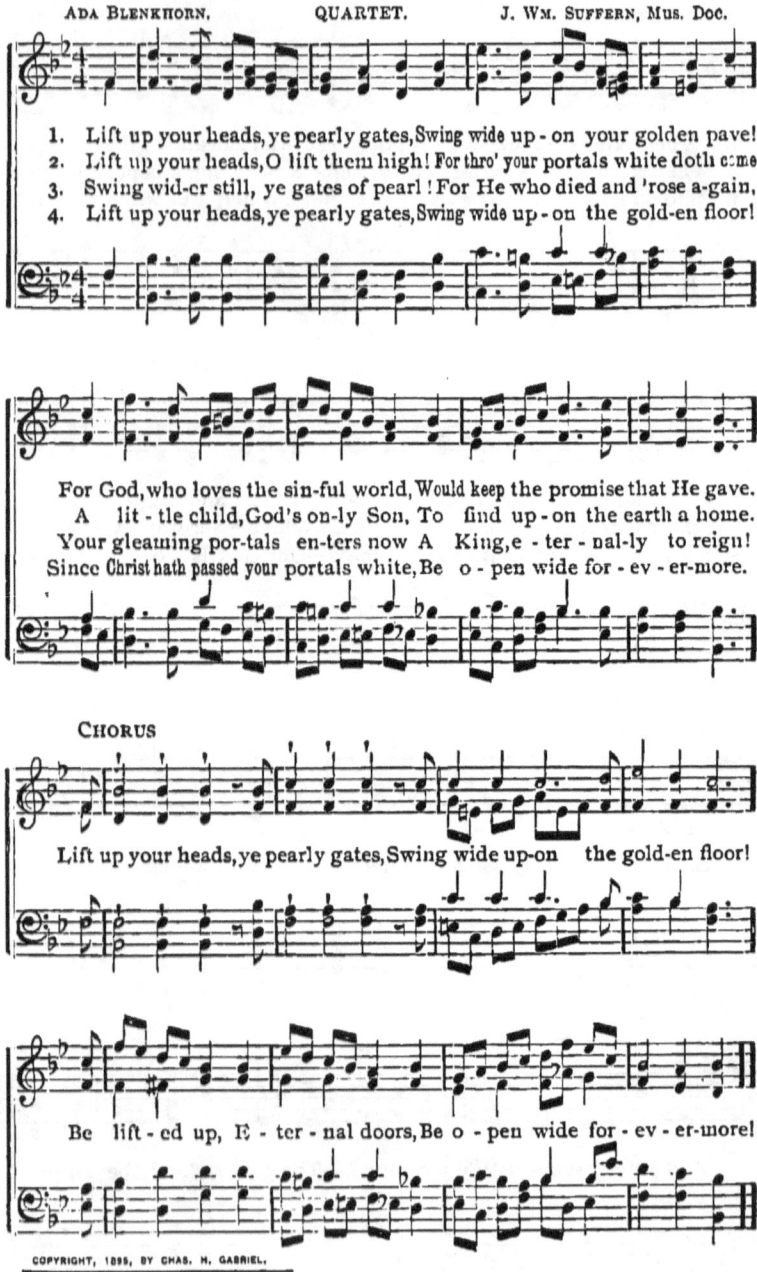

Sound It Out With Singing.

No. 188. I AM TRUSTING, LORD, IN THEE.

Rev. WM. McDONALD.   WM. G. FISCHER.

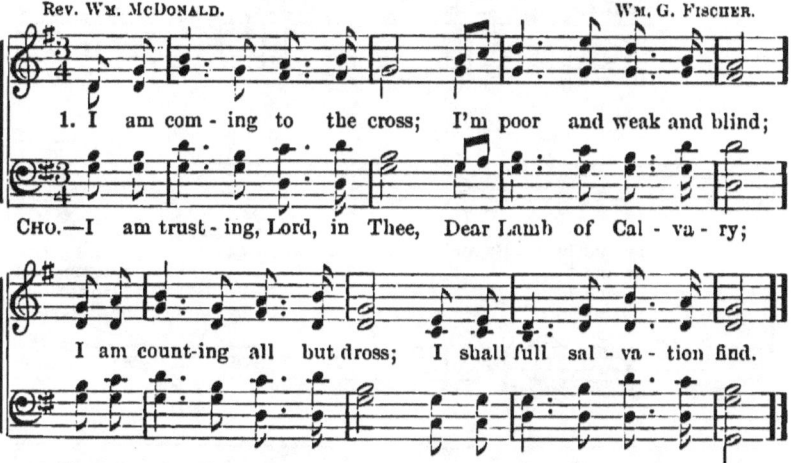

2 Long my heart has sighed for Thee;
   Long has evil dwelt within;
 Jesus sweetly speaks to me,
   I will cleanse you from all sin.

3 Here I give my all to Thee,—
   Friends and time and earthly store,
 Soul and body Thine to be—
   Wholly Thine—forevermore.

4 In the promises I trust;
   In the cleansing blood confide;

I am prostrate in the dust;
   I with Christ am crucified.

5 Jesus comes! He fills my soul!
   Perfected in love I am;
 I am every whit made whole;
   Glory, glory to the Lamb!
    (Chorus to 5th verse.)
 Still I'm trusting, Lord, in Thee,
   Dear Lamb of Calvary;
 Humbly at Thy cross I bow—
   Jesus saves me! saves me now.

BY PERMISSION.

No. 191. **PRAISE THE LORD.**

Mrs. Ida M. Budd. Chas. H. Gabriel.

1. In the dawn-ing of the morning, when the crystal dew is shin-ing,
2. In the sul-try hour of noon-day, when the hearts and hands are weary
3. In the qui-et hush of ev-'ning, when we're free from care and la-bor,
4. Then at dawn, or noon, or ev-'ning, we will ev - er sing His prais-es,

And the birds their joy-ous mat-ins pour up - on the fra-grant air,
With the toil - ing, and the bur-den, and the fer-vent sum-mer heat,
When the gold - en sun is sink-ing in his pur - ple cloud-y sea,
And His love shall be our sto - ry and our ev - er - last-ing theme,

We will praise our lov-ing Fa-ther who has shown a - new His mer-cy,
We will praise Him for His promise of a rest in heav'n re-main-ing,
We will of - fer our thanksgiving to the Giv - er of all bless-ings,
Till a-mong the just, made per-fect, we shall join the hap - py cho-rus

And thro' all the hours of darkness still has kept us in His care.
And of past-ures where a Shepherd kind shall lead our will-ing feet.
Praising Him for bless-ed free-dom wherein Christ has made us free.
The tri - umph-ant hosts are sing-ing on the banks of Jordan's stream.

COPYRIGHT, 1894, BY CHAS. H. GABRIEL.

Praise the Lord.

No. 192. WORK FOR THE NIGHT.
Key of F.

1 Work, for the night is coming;
  Work through the morning hours;
  Work, while the dew is sparkling;
  Work, 'mid springing flowers;
  Work, when the day grows brighter,
  Work, in the glowing sun:
  Work, for the night is coming,
  When man's work is done.

2 Work, for the night is coming;
  Work through the sunny noon
  Fill brightest hours with labor;
  Rest comes sure and soon.
  Give every flying minute
  Something to keep in store;
  Work, for the night is coming,
  When man works no more.

3 Work, for the night is coming,
  Under the sunset skies;
  While their bright tints are glowing,
  Work, for daylight flies.
  Work, till the last beam fadeth,
  Fadeth to shine no more;
  Work, while the night is dark'ning,
  When man's work is o'er.

No. 193. STAND UP FOR JESUS.
Tune:—WEBB.

1 Stand up! stand up for Jesus!
  Ye soldiers of the cross;
  Lift high His royal banner,
  It must not suffer loss;
  From victory unto victory
  His army He shall lead,
  Till every foe is vanquished,
  And Christ is Lord indeed.

2 Stand up! stand up for Jesus!
  Stand in His strength alone;
  The arm of flesh will fail you—
  Ye dare not trust your own;
  Put on the gospel armor,
  And, watching unto prayer,
  Where duty calls, or danger,
  Be never wanting there.

3 Stand up! stand up for Jesus!
  The strife will not be long;
  This day the noise of battle,
  The next the victor's song;
  To him that overcometh,
  A crown of life shall be;
  He with the King of glory
  Shall reign eternally.

No. 205. COME, LET US JOIN.

1. Come, let us join our cheerful songs With angels round the throne;
2. "Worthy the Lamb that died," they cry, "To be exalted thus!"
3. Jesus is worthy to receive Honor and pow'r divine;
4. Let all that dwell above the sky, And air, and earth, and seas,
5. The whole creation join in one, To bless the sacred name

Ten thousand thousand are their tongues, But all their joys are one.
"Worthy the Lamb!" our lips reply, "For He was slain for us."
And blessings, more than we can give, Be, Lord, for ever Thine!
Conspire to lift Thy glories high, And speak Thine endless praise.
Of Him who sits upon the throne And to adore the Lamb!

No. 206. HARK! TEN THOUSAND.

1. { Hark! ten thousand harps and voices, Sound the note of praise above;
   Jesus reigns, and heav'n rejoices, Jesus reigns, the God of love, }
2. { Jesus, hail! whose glory brightens, All above, and gives it worth;
   Lord of life, Thy smile enlightens, Cheers and charms Thy saints on earth. }

D.C.—Hallelujah, Hallelujah! Hallelujah, Amen.

See, He sits on yonder throne; Jesus rules the world alone;
When we think of love like Thine, Lord, we own it love divine;

3 King of glory reign forever;
  Thine an everlasting crown;
Nothing from Thy love shall sever
  Those whom Thou hast made Thine own;
Happy objects of Thy grace,
  Destined to behold Thy face.

4 Savior, hasten Thine appearing;
  Bring, oh, bring the glorious day,
When, the awful summons hearing,
  Heaven and earth shall pass away;
Then with golden harps we'll sing,
  "Glory, glory to our King."

No. 207. THE SINNER INVITED.

2 Where the saints rob'd in white,
  Cleans'd in life's flowing fountain,
  Shining beauteous and bright,
  They inhabit the mountain.
  Where no sin nor dismay,
  Neither trouble nor sorrow,
  Will be felt for a day,
  Nor be fear'd for the morrow.

3 He's prepared thee a home—
  Sinner, canst thou believe it?
  And invites thee to come.
  Sinner, wilt thou receive it?
  O come, sinner, come,
  For the tide is receding,
  And the Savior will soon
  And forever cease pleading.

No. 208. LEIGHTON. S. M.

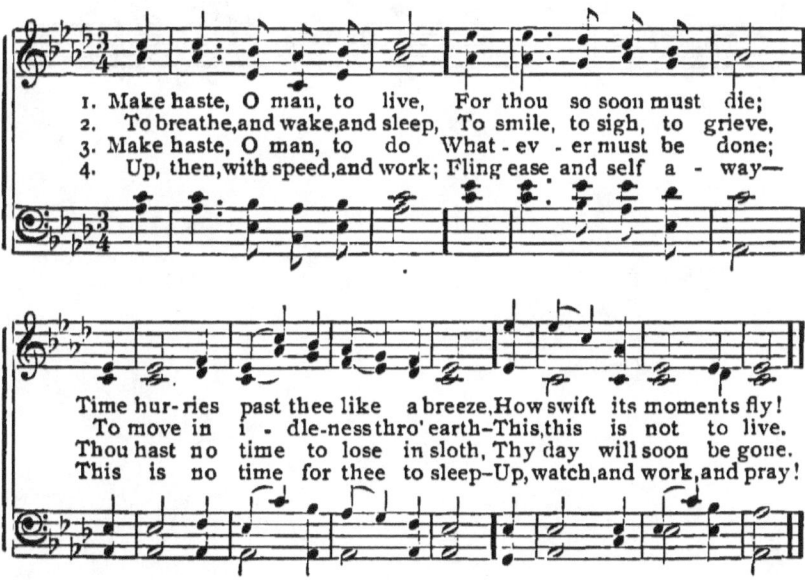

No. 209. MY JESUS, AS THOU WILT.

1. My Jesus, as Thou wilt: O may Thy will be mine; Into Thy hand of love I would my all resign. Thro' sorrow or thro' joy, Conduct me as Thine own, And help me still to say, "My Lord, Thy will be done."

2. My Jesus, as Thou wilt: Tho' seen thro' many a tear, Let not my star of hope Grow dim or disappear. Since Thou on earth hast wept And sorrow'd oft alone, If I must weep with Thee, My Lord, Thy will be done.

3. My Jesus, as Thou wilt: All shall be well for me; Each changing future scene I gladly trust with Thee. Straight to my home above, I travel calmly on, And sing in life or death, "My Lord, Thy will be done."

America.

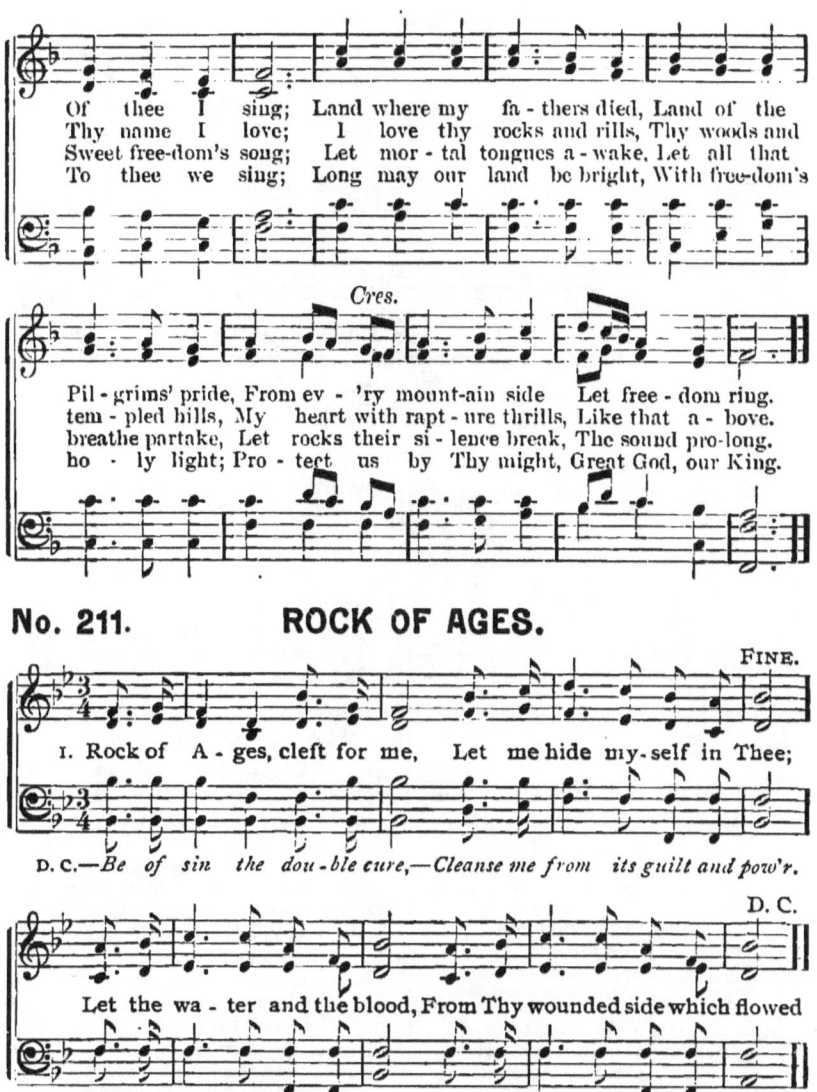

Of thee I sing; Land where my fa-thers died, Land of the Pil-grims' pride, From ev-'ry mount-ain side Let free-dom ring.
Thy name I love; I love thy rocks and rills, Thy woods and tem-pled hills, My heart with rapt-ure thrills, Like that a-bove.
Sweet free-dom's song; Let mor-tal tongues a-wake, Let all that breathe partake, Let rocks their si-lence break, The sound pro-long.
To thee we sing; Long may our land be bright, With free-dom's ho-ly light; Pro-tect us by Thy might, Great God, our King.

No. 211. ROCK OF AGES.

1. Rock of A-ges, cleft for me, Let me hide my-self in Thee;
Let the wa-ter and the blood, From Thy wounded side which flowed

D. C.—Be of sin the dou-ble cure,—Cleanse me from its guilt and pow'r.

2 Not the labor of my hands
Can fulfil the law's demands;
Could my zeal no respite know,
Could my tears forever flow,
All for sin could not atone,—
Thou must save, and Thou alone.

3 Nothing in my hand I bring;
Simply to Thy cross I cling;
Naked, come to Thee for dress,

Helpless, look to Thee for grace,—
Vile, I to the Fountain fly,
Wash me, Savior, or I die.

4 While I draw this fleeting breath,
When my heart-strings break in death,
When I soar to worlds unknown,
See Thee on Thy judgment throne,
Rock of Ages, cleft for me,
Let me hide myself in Thee.

No. 212. COME, MY SOUL.

1. Come, my soul, thy suit prepare, Jesus loves to answer pray'r;
He Himself invites thee near, Bids thee ask Him, waits to hear.

2. Lord, I come to Thee for rest; Take possession of my breast;
There Thy blood-bought right maintain, And without a rival reign.

3 While I am a pilgrim here,
Let Thy love my spirit cheer;
As my Guide, my Guard, my Friend,
Lead me to my journey's end.

4 Show me what I have to do;
Every hour my strength renew:
Let me live a life of faith,
Let me die Thy people's death.

No. 213.
Children of the Heavenly King.

1 Children of the heavenly King,
As we journey we will sing,—
Sing our Savior's worthy praise,
Glorious in His works and ways.

2 We are traveling home to God,
In the way the fathers trod;
They are happy now, and we
Soon their happiness shall see.

3 O ye mourning souls, be glad,
Christ our advocate is made;
Us to save our flesh assumes,
Brother to our souls becomes.

4 Shout, ye little flock, and blest,
Soon we'll enter into rest;
There our seat is now prepared,
There our Kingdom and reward.

5 Lord, submissive make us go,
Gladly leaving all below;
Only Thou our leader be,
And we still will follow Thee.

No. 214. Hark, My Soul.

1 Hark, my soul, it is the Lord;
'Tis thy Savior, hear His word;
Jesus speaks, and speaks to thee,
"Say, poor sinner, lovest thou me?

2 "I delivered thee when bound,
And, when wounded, healed thy wound;
Sought thee wandering, set thee right,
Turned thy darkness into light.

3 Can a woman's tender care
Cease toward the child she bare?
Yes, she may forgetful be,
Yet will I remember thee.

4 Mine is an unchanging love,
Higher than the heights above,
Deeper than the depths beneath,
Free and faithful, strong as death.

5 Thou shalt see my glory soon,
When the work of grace is done;
Partner of my throne shalt be;
Say, poor sinner, lovest thou me?"

6 Lord, it is my chief complaint,
That my love is weak and faint;
Yet I love Thee and adore,
Oh, for grace to love Thee more!

No. 215. ROOM FOR ALL.

L. B. Bates.   C. H. G.

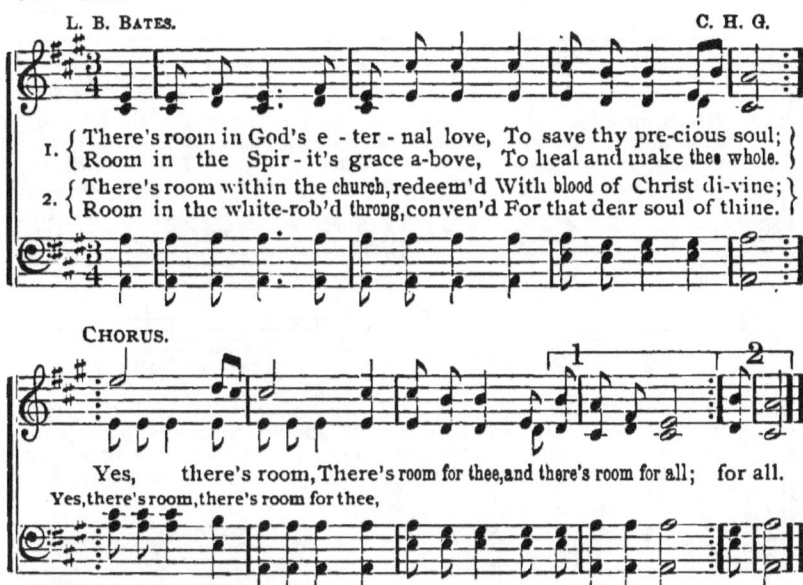

1. There's room in God's e-ter-nal love, To save thy pre-cious soul;
Room in the Spir-it's grace a-bove, To heal and make thee whole.
2. There's room within the church, redeem'd With blood of Christ di-vine;
Room in the white-rob'd throng, conven'd For that dear soul of thine.

CHORUS.
Yes, there's room, There's room for thee, and there's room for all; for all.
Yes, there's room, there's room for thee,

COPYRIGHT, 1894, BY CHAS. H. GABRIEL.

3. There's room in heav'n among the choir,
And harps and crowns of gold,
And glorious palms of vict'ry there,
And joys that ne'er were told.

4. There's room around thy Father's board
For thee and millions more;
Oh, come and welcome to the Lord,
Yea, come this very hour.

AZMON.

No. 216.

1 Oh, for a heart to praise my God,
A heart from sin set free!
A heart that always feels Thy blood
So freely spilt for me!

2 A heart resigned, submissive, meek,
My great Redeemer's throne;
Where only Christ is heard to speak,
Where Jesus reigns alone.

3 A heart in every thought renewed,
And full of love divine;
Perfect, and right, and pure, and good,
A copy, Lord, of Thine.

No. 217.

1 Salvation! Oh, the joyful sound!
What pleasure to our ears;
A sovereign balm for every wound
A cordial for our fears.

2 Salvation! let the echo fly
The spacious earth around,
While all the armies of the sky
Conspire to raise the sound.

3 Salvation! O Thou bleeding Lamb!
To Thee the praise belongs;
Salvation shall inspire our hearts,
And dwell upon our tongues.

No. 218. THE FIRM FOUNDATION.

5 "E'en down to old age all my people shall prove [love;
My sovereign, eternal, unchangeable
And when hoary hairs shall their temples adorn, [be borne.
Like lambs they shall still in my bosom

6 "The soul that on Jesus hath leaned for repose,
I will not, I will not desert to his foes;
That soul, though all hell should endeavor to shake,
I'll never, no never, no never forsake!"

No. 219. SAVIOR, PILOT ME.

1. Je-sus, Sav-ior, pi-lot me O-ver life's tem-pest-uous sea;
Chart and com-pass came from Thee: Je-sus, Sav-ior, pi-lot me.

Unknown waves be-fore me roll, Hid-ing rock and treacherous shoal;

2 When the apostle's fragile bark
  Struggled with the billow's dark.
  On the stormy Galilee,
  Thou didst walk upon the sea;
  And when they beheld Thy form,
  Safe they glided through the storm.

3 As a mother stills her child,
  Thou canst hush the ocean wild;
  Boisterous waves obey Thy will

When Thou sayest to them, "Be still!"
Wondrous Sovereign of the sea,
Jesus, Savior, pilot me.

4 When at last I near the shore,
  And the fearful breakers roar
  'Twixt me and the peaceful rest,
  Then, while leaning on Thy breast,
  May I hear Thee say to me,
  "Fear not, I will pilot thee!"

No. 220. I Gave My Life.

1 I gave my life for thee,
    My precious blood I shed,
  That thou might'st ransomed be,
    And quickened from the dead.
  ‖: I gave, I gave my life for thee, :‖
    What hast thou given for me?

2 My Father's house of light,
    My glory-circled throne
  I left, for earthly night,
    For wand'rings sad and lone.
  ‖: I left, I left it all for thee, :‖
    Hast thou left aught for me?

3 I suffered much for thee,
    More than my tongue can tell,
  Of bitterest agony,
    To rescue thee from hell;
  ‖: I've borne, I've borne it all for thee, :‖
    What hast thou borne for me?

4 And I have brought to thee,
    Down from my home above,
  Salvation full and free,
    My pardon and my love;
  ‖: I bring, I bring rich gifts to thee, :‖
    What hast thou brought to me?

F. R. HAVERGAL.

No. 221. Take The Name Of Jesus.

Key, A♭

1 Take the name of Jesus with you,
    Child of sorrow and of woe;
  It will joy and comfort give you,
    Take it, then, where'er you go.

Cho.—Precious name, O how sweet,
    Hope of earth and joy of heaven;
  Precious name, O how sweet,
    Hope of earth and joy of heaven.

2 Take the name of Jesus ever,
    As a shield from every snare;
  If temptations round you gather,
    Breathe that holy name in prayer.

3 Oh! the precious name of Jesus;
    How it thrills our souls with joy,
  When His loving arms receive us,
    And His songs our tongues employ.

4 At the name of Jesus bowing,
    Falling prostrate at His feet,
  King of kings in heav'n we'll crown Him,
    When our journey is complete.

Mrs. LYDIA BAXTER.

No. 222. O DAY OF REST AND GLADNESS.

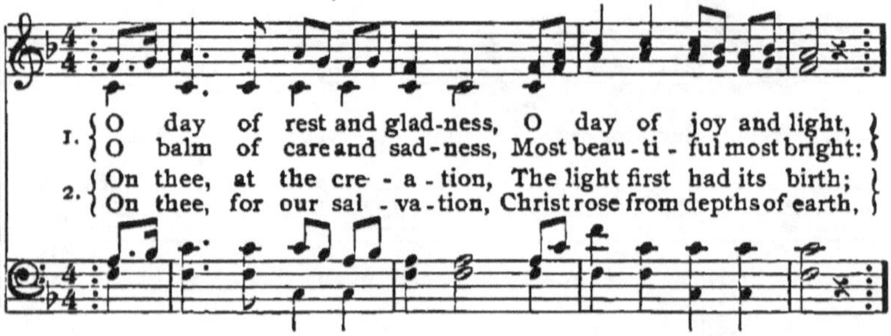

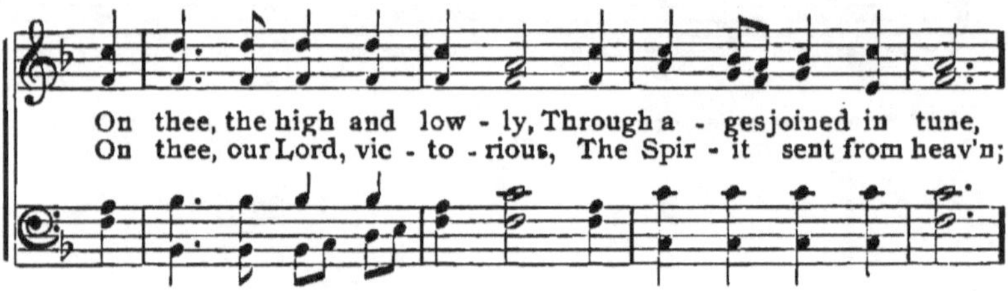

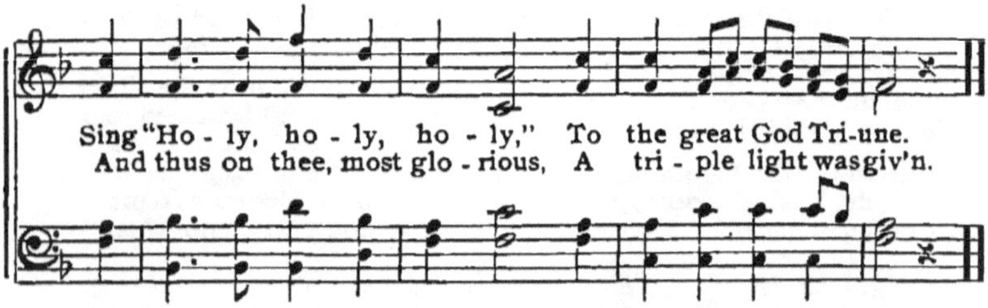

1. O day of rest and gladness, O day of joy and light,
O balm of care and sadness, Most beautiful most bright:
On thee, the high and lowly, Through ages joined in tune,
Sing "Holy, holy, holy," To the great God Triune.

2. On thee, at the creation, The light first had its birth;
On thee, for our salvation, Christ rose from depths of earth,
On thee, our Lord, victorious, The Spirit sent from heav'n;
And thus on thee, most glorious, A triple light was giv'n.

3 To-day on weary nations
   The heavenly manna falls,
To holy convocations
   The silver trumpet calls,
Where gospel light is glowing
   With pure and radiant beams,
And living water flowing
   With soul-refreshing streams.

4 New graces ever gaining
   From this our day of rest,
We reach the rest remaining
   To spirits of the blest;
To Holy Ghost be praises,
   To Father, and to Son;
The Church her voice upraises
   To Thee, blest Three in One.

No. 223. JESUS IS MINE!

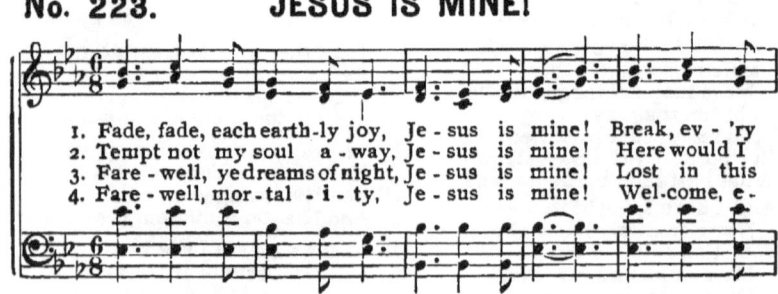

1. Fade, fade, each earthly joy, Jesus is mine! Break, ev-'ry
2. Tempt not my soul away, Jesus is mine! Here would I
3. Farewell, ye dreams of night, Jesus is mine! Lost in this
4. Farewell, mortality, Jesus is mine! Welcome, e-

Jesus Is Mine.

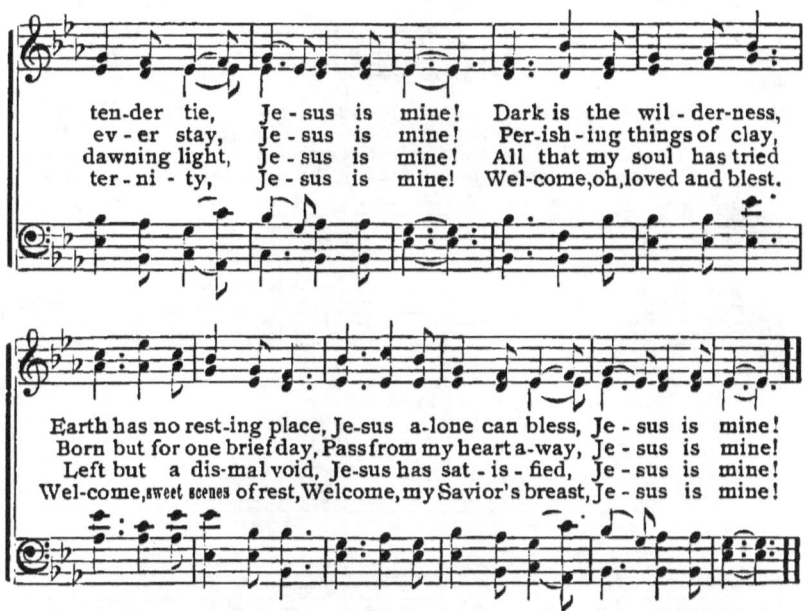

No. 224. I STRETCH MY HANDS TO THEE.

CHARLES WESLEY. Tune: I DO BELIEVE, C. M.

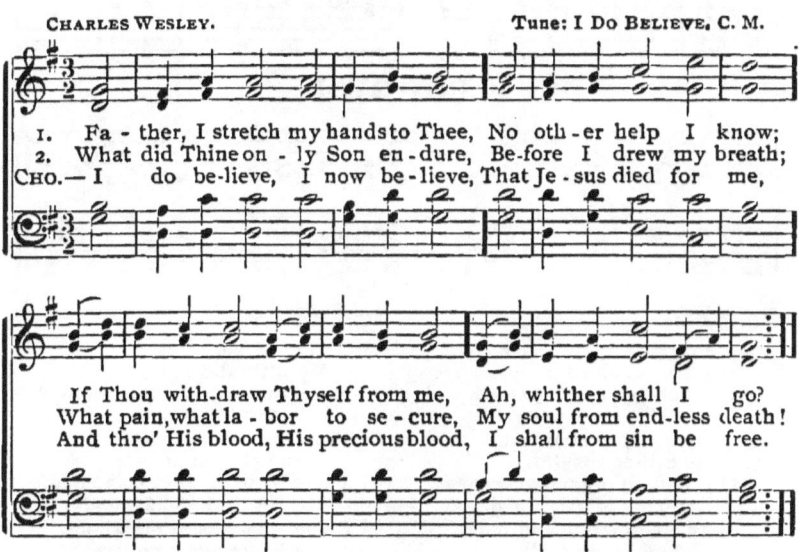

3 O Jesus, could I this believe,
  I now should feel Thy power;
  And all my wants Thou wouldst re-
  In this accepted hour. [lieve.

4 Author of faith, to Thee I lift
  My weary, longing eyes;
  O let me now receive that gift!
  My soul without it dies.

No. 225. CONSECRATION.

Mrs. Mary D. James.   Mrs. Jos. F. Knapp.

1. My body, soul and spirit, Jesus, I give to Thee, A consecrated offering, Thine evermore to be.
2. O Jesus, mighty Savior, I trust in Thy great name, I look for Thy salvation, Thy promise now I claim.
3. Oh, let the fire, descending Just now upon my soul, Consume my humble offering, And cleanse and make me whole.
4. I'm Thine, O blessed Jesus, Wash'd by Thy precious blood, Now seal me by Thy Spirit, A sacrifice to God.

REFRAIN.
My all is on the altar, I'm waiting for the fire; Waiting, waiting, waiting. I'm waiting for the fire.

BOYLSTON.

No. 226.

1 A charge to keep I have;
  A God to glorify:
  A never-dying soul to save,
  And fit it for the sky.

2 To serve the present age,
  My calling to fulfill,
  O may it all my powers engage
  To do my Master's will.

3 Help me to watch and pray,
  And on Thyself rely;
  Assured if I my trust betray,
  I shall forever die.

No. 227.

1 And can I yet delay
  My little all to give?
  To tear my soul from earth away,
  For Jesus to receive?

2 Nay, but I yield, I yield!
  I can hold out no more:
  I sink by dying love compell'd,
  And own the Conqueror!

3 Come, and possess me whole,
  Nor hence again remove;
  Settle and fix my wavering soul
  With all Thy weight of love.

No. 228. MUST JESUS BEAR THE CROSS.

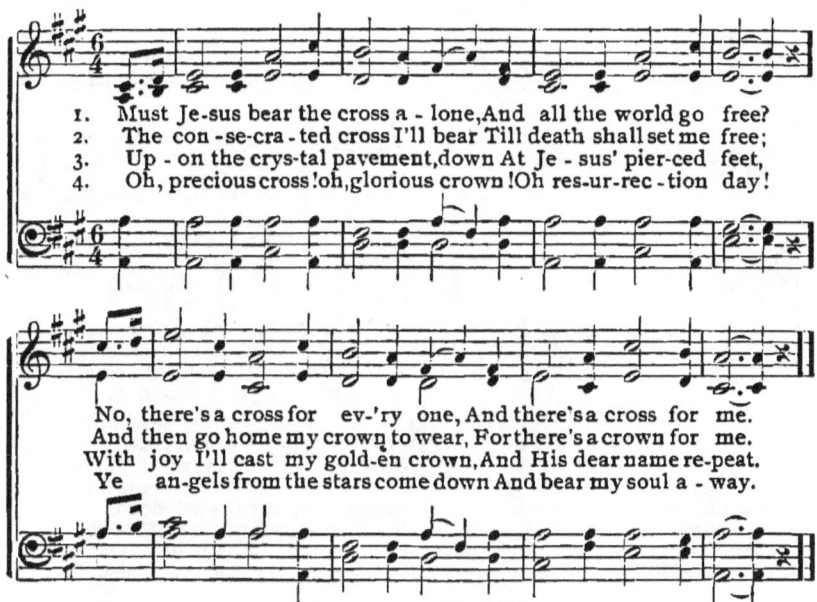

1. Must Jesus bear the cross alone, And all the world go free?
2. The consecrated cross I'll bear Till death shall set me free;
3. Upon the crystal pavement, down At Jesus' pierced feet,
4. Oh, precious cross! oh, glorious crown! Oh resurrection day!

No, there's a cross for ev'ry one, And there's a cross for me.
And then go home my crown to wear, For there's a crown for me.
With joy I'll cast my golden crown, And His dear name repeat.
Ye angels from the stars come down And bear my soul away.

No. 229.
I Love to Tell the Story.
Key of A♭.

1 I love to tell the story
  Of unseen things above,
Of Jesus and His glory,
  Of Jesus and His love.
I love to tell the story,
  Because I know 'tis true;
It satisfies my longings
  As nothing else can do.

CHO.—I love to tell the story,
  'Twill be my theme in glory,
To tell the old, old story
  Of Jesus and His love.

2 I love to tell the story:
  More wonderful it seems
Than all the golden fancies
  Of all our golden dreams.
I love to tell the story,
  It did so much for me;
And that is just the reason,
  I tell it now to thee.

3 I love to tell the story,
  For those who know it best
Seem hungering and thirsting
  To hear it like the rest.
And when, in scenes of glory,
  I sing the new, new song,
'Twill be the old, old story
  That I have loved so long.
                CATERINE HANKEY.

No. 230.
Marching to Zion.
Key of G.

1 Come, ye that love the Lord,
  And let your joys be known,
Join in a song with sweet accord,
Join in a song with sweet accord,
  And thus surround the throne,
  And thus surround the throne.

CHO.—We're marching to Zion,
  Beautiful, beautiful Zion,
We're marching upward to Zion,
  The beautiful city of God.

2 Let those refuse to sing
  Who never knew our God;
But children of the heav'nly King,
But children of the heav'nly King,
  May speak their joys abroad.
  May speak their joys abroad.

3 The hill of Zion yields,
  A thousand sacred sweets,
Before we reach the heav'nly fields,
Before we reach the heav'nly fields,
  Or walk the golden streets,
  Or walk the golden streets.

4 Then let our songs abound,
  And every tear be dry,
We're marching through Immanuel's [ground,
We're marching through Immanuel's [ground,
  To fairer worlds on high,
  To fairer worlds on high.
                ISAAC WATTS.

No. 231. HOLY SPIRIT, FAITHFUL GUIDE.

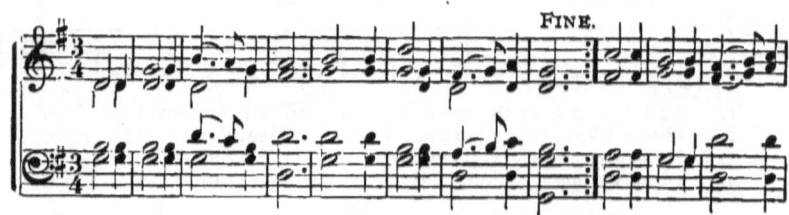

1 Holy Spirit, faithful Guide,
Ever near the Christian's side,
Gently lead us by the hand,
Pilgrims in a desert land.
Weary souls, fore'er rejoice,
While they hear that sweetest voice
Whispering softly, "Wanderer, come,
Follow me, I'll guide thee home."

2 Ever present, truest Friend,
Ever near, Thine aid to lend,
Leave us not to doubt and fear,
Groping on in darkness drear.
When the storms are raging sore,
Hearts grow faint, and hopes give o'er,
Whisper softly, "Wanderer, come,
Follow me, I'll guide thee home."

3 When our days of toil shall cease,
Waiting still for sweet release,
Nothing left but heaven and prayer,
Wondering if our names are there;
Wading deep the dismal flood,
Pleading naught but Jesus' blood;
Wisper softly, "Wanderer, come,
Follow me, I'll guide thee home."

No. 232. WHAT A FRIEND.

1 What a friend we have in Jesus,
　All our sins and griefs to bear!
What a privilege to carry
　Everything to God in prayer!
Oh, what peace we often forfeit,
Oh, what needless pain we bear,
All because we do not carry
　Everything to God in prayer!

2 Have we trials and temptations?
　Is there trouble anywhere?
We should never be discouraged,
　Take it to the Lord in prayer.
Can we find a friend so faithful,
　Who will all our sorrows share?
Jesus knows our every weakness,
　Take it to the Lord in prayer.

3 Are we weak and heavy laden,
　Cumbered with a load of care,
Precious Savior, still our refuge,
　Take it to the Lord in prayer.
Do thy friends despise, forsake thee?
　Take it to the Lord in prayer:
In His arms He'll take and shield thee,
Thou wilt find a solace there.

No. 233. Jesus, my All.

1 Jesus, my all, to heaven is gone,
He whom I fix my hopes upon;
His track I see, and I'll pursue
The narrow way, till Him I view,
The way the holy prophets went,
The road that leads from banishment,
The Kings highway of holiness,
I'll go, for all His paths are peace.

2 This is the way I long have sought,
And mourned, because I found it not;
My grief a burden long has been,
Because I was not saved from sin.
The more I strove against its power,
I felt its weight and guilt the more;
'Till late I heard my Savior say
"Come hither, soul, I am the way."

3 Lo! glad I come; and Thou, blest lamb,
Shalt take me to Thee as I am;
Nothing but sin have I to give;
Nothing but love shall I receive.
Then will I tell to sinners 'round,
What a dear Savior I have found,
I'll point to Thy redeeming blood,
And say, "Behold the way to God."

No 234. Tell it to Jesus.

1 Are you weary, are you heavy-hearted,
Tell it to Jesus, tell it to Jesus;
Are you grieving over joys departed?
Tell it to Jesus alone.

CHO.—Tell it to Jesus, tell it to Jesus,
He is a friend that's well known;
You have no other such a friend or brother,
Tell it to Jesus alone.

2 Do the tears flow down your cheeks
unbidden?
Tell it to Jesus, tell it to Jesus; [den?
Have you sins that to man's eye are hid-
Tell it to Jesus alone.

3 Do you fear the gathering clouds of
sorrow?
Tell it to Jesus, tell it to Jesus; [row?
Are you anxious what shall be tomor-
Tell it to Jesus alone.

4 Are you troubled at the tho't of dying?
Tell it to Jesus, tell it to Jesus;
For Christ's coming kingdom are you
sighing?
Tell it to Jesus alone.

No. 235. The Lily of the Valley.

1 I have found a friend in Jesus, He's
every thing to me,
He's the fairest of ten thousand to
my soul;
The Lily of the Valley, in Him alone
I see,
All I need to cleanse and make me
fully whole;
In sorrow He's my comfort, in trouble
He's my stay,
He tells me every care on Him to roll,
He's the Lily of the Valley, the bright
and Morning Star,
He's the fairest of ten thousand to my
soul.

CHO.—In sorrow He's my comfort, in
trouble He's my stay,
He tells me every care on Him to roll.
He's the Lily of the Valley, the bright
and Morning Star,
He's the fairest of ten thousand to my
soul.

2 He all my griefs has taken, and all my
sorrows borne;
In temptation He's my strong and
mighty tower;
I have all for Him forsaken, and all
idols torn
From my heart, and now He keeps
me by His power.
Though all the world forsake me and
Satan tempts me sore, [goal.
Thro' Jesus I shall safely reach the
He's the Lily of the Valley, the bright
and Morning Star,
He's the fairest of ten thousand to my
soul.

3 He will never, never leave me, nor yet
forsake me here,
While I live by faith and do His bless-
ed will;
A wall of fire about me, I've nothing
now to fear;
With His manna He my hungry soul
shall fill;
Then sweeping up to glory we see His
blessed face,
Where rivers of delight shall ever roll,
He's the Lily of the Valley, the bright
and Morning Star,
He's the fairest of ten thousand to my
soul.

No. 236. Blessed be the name.

1 All praise to Him who reigns above,
  In majesty supreme;
  Who gave His Son for man to die,
  That He might man redeem.
Cho.—Blessed be the name, blessed be the
  Blessed be the name of the Lord; [name,
  Blessed be the name, blessed be the name,
  Blessed be the name of the Lord.

2 His name above all names shall stand,
  Exalted more and more,
  At God the Father's own right hand,
  Where angel hosts adore.

3 Redeemer, Savior, Friend of man,
  Once ruined by the fall,
  Thou hast devised salvation's plan,
  For Thou hast died for all.

4 His name shall be the Counselor,
  The mighty Prince of Peace,
  Of all earth's kingdom's Conqueror,
  Whose reign shall never cease.

5 The ransomed hosts to Thee shall bring
  Their praise and homage meet;
  With rapturous awe adore their King,
  And worship at His feet.

No. 237. The Home Over There.

1 Oh, think of the home over there,
  By the side of the river of light,
  Where the saints, all immortal and fair,
  Are robed in their garments of white.
Ref.—Over there, over there,
  Oh, think of the home over there.

2 Oh, think of the friends over there,
  Who before us the journey have trod,
  Of the songs that they breathe on the air,
  In their home in the palace of God.
Ref.—Over there, over there,
  Oh, think of the friends over there.

3 My Savior is now over there, [rest;
  There my kindred and friends are at
  Then away from my sorrow and care,
  Let me fly to the land of the blest.
Ref.—Over there, over there,
  My Savior is now over there.

4 I'll soon be at home over there,
  For the end of my journey I see;
  Many dear to my heart, over there,
  Are watching and waiting for me
Ref.—Over there, over there,
  I'll soon be at home over there.

No. 238. Nearer, my God.

1 Nearer, my God, to Thee!
  Nearer to Thee,
  E'en though it be a cross
  That raiseth me;
  Still all my song shall be,
  Nearer, my God, to Thee,
  Nearer to Thee!

2 Though like a wanderer
  The sun gone down,
  Darkness be over me,
  My rest a stone,
  Yet in my dreams I'd be
  Nearer, my God, to Thee,
  Nearer to Thee!

3 There let the way appear,
  Steps unto Heaven;
  All that Thou sendest me,
  In mercy given;
  Angels to beckon me
  Nearer, my God, to Thee,
  Nearer to Thee!

4 Then, with my waking thoughts
  Bright with Thy praise,
  Out of my stony griefs
  Bethel I'll raise;
  So by my woes to be
  Nearer, my God, to Thee,
  Nearer to Thee!

5 Or if, on joyful wing
  Cleaving the sky,
  Sun, moon, and stars forgot,
  Upward I fly,
  Still all my song shall be,
  Nearer, my God, to Thee,
  Nearer to Thee!

No. 239. Blessed Assurance.

1 Blessed assurance, Jesus is mine!
  Oh, what a foretaste of glory divine!
  Heir of salvation, purchase of God,
  Born of His Spirit, washed in His blood.
Cho.—||:This is my story, this is my song,
  Praising the Savior all the day long:||

2 Perfect submission, perfect delight,
  Visions of rapture burst forth on my sight,
  Angels descending, bring from above
  Echoes of mercy, whispers of love.

3 Perfect submission, all is at rest,
  I in my Savior am happy and blest,
  Watching and waiting and looking above,
  Filled with His goodness, lost in His love.

INDEX.

Titles in SMALL CAPITALS. First lines in Roman.

A

	No.
A charge to keep I have	226
A hymn of praise to-day	44
A LOYAL BAND	93
A PERFECT HEART	58
A PLACE AND WORK FOR ME	40
A REASONABLE SERVICE	78
AFTERWARD	76
All hail the power of Jesus' name	121
All praise to Him who reigns above	236
All the palace gates are open	36
ALL THE WAY	17
All things are ready, come to the feast	198
AMERICA	210
Amid the trials which I meet	203
And can I yet delay	227
ANYWHERE WITH JESUS	143
Are you peaceful in your hearts	187
Are you weary, are you heavy laden	234
Are you walking in the highway	129
Art thou sitting by the wayside	102
As a pilgrim band bound for Canaan's	59
As, in weakness, you are pressing	23
As our heavenly Father the sparrow's	199
As thou once the host preceded	197
AT HOME FOREVER	157
AZMON	216

B

	No.
BATTLE HYMN OF MISSIONS	95
BE A GOLDEN SUNBEAM	73
BE CAREFUL	134
BEAUTIFUL LOVE	43
BEAUTIFUL RAIMENT	144
BLESSED ASSURANCE	239
BLESSED BE THE NAME	236
BLESSED JESUS	65
BLESSED PEACE	16
BLESSED SUNLIGHT	15
Blest be the tie that binds	175
BOYLSTON	226
BRING THEM TO JESUS	109
Brother, hast thou wandered	49
BY FAITH I FOLLOW ON	170

C

	No.
Can I be silent, when I know	159
CAN IT BE	122
CAN YOU DOUBT HIM	155
Carry the message to lands far away	94
CHILDREN OF THE HEAV'NLY KING	213
CHIME ON, SWEET BELLS	11
CHRIST, AND CHRIST ALONE	194
CHRIST IS PASSING BY	102
Christ, of all my hopes the ground	114
COME, HOLY SPIRIT	77
COME, LET US JOIN	205
Come, let us join our cheerful songs	90
COME, MY SOUL	212
COME, POWER OF GOD	156
COME, THOU ALMIGHTY KING	165
COME THOU, O TRAVELER	103
COME TO THE FEAST	198
Come to the precious Gospel feast	75
Come ye that love the Lord	230
CONQUERING GRACE	162
CONSECRATION	225
CORONATION	121

D

	No.
DARE TO DO RIGHT	9
Dare to think, tho' others frown	9
DELAY NOT	35
DENNIS	175
DEPTH OF MERCY	115
Do life's cares and burdens oft	119
Do we want to go to heaven	135
DRAW NEAR, O COMFORTER	190

E

	No.
ENOUGH FOR THEE AND ME	159
Eternal Father, thou hast said	95

F

	No.
Fade, fade, each earthly joy	223
Father, I stretch my hands to thee	224
Forever with the Lord	185
For the beauty of the earth	83
FOR THE RIGHT	179
Forward, Christian soldier true	108
Forward, ever forward	64
FORWARD GO	108
FROM GREENLAND'S ICY MOUNTAINS	204
From the cross of Christ uplifted	120
From the rising	46

INDEX

G

	No.
GATHER IN THE GRAIN	27
GENTLY LEAD US	147
Gently, Lord, oh, gently lead us	147
GET FACE TO FACE WITH JESUS	33
GLAD TIDINGS	168
GLORIOUS NEWS	94
GLORY FOR ME	70
GOD'S MANSIONS ARE OPEN	126
Go forth to the work	82
Go, gather in the golden grain	27

H

	No.
Hail to the brightness of Zion's glad	146
HAPPY IN MY SAVIOR	48
HARK! MY SOUL	214
HARK! TEN THOUSAND	206
HEAVENLY REST	185
HE CARES FOR ME	176
HE CARETH FOR ME	200
HE HIDETH ME	61
HE IS COMING AGAIN	171
HE KNOWETH	182
HE LEADETH ME	56
HE SAVES ME, I KNOW	140
HE SAVES ME TO-DAY	111
He's my shepherd, why should I	176
HERE AM I	88
Holy Father, send thy blessing	37
HOLY SPIRIT, FAITHFUL GUIDE	231
HOME, HOME, SWEET HOME	181
How can I come to the Savior	117
How firm a foundation, ye saints	218
How I long to be there	70
HURSLEY	161

I

	No.
I am coming to the cross	188
I AM THINE, AND THOU ART MINE	12
I am thine, O Lord, thou hast called	12
I AM TRUSTING, LORD, IN THEE	188
I am walking to-day	41
I CAN ALWAYS TRUST HIM	163
I can hear my Savior calling	139
I CAN TRUST THEE	67
I GAVE MY LIFE FOR THEE	220
I have found a friend in Jesus	235
I have heard the story of redeeming	162
I have read of the sweet, olden story	22
I have sinned, O God, My Savior	97
I hear them sing of Jesus	122
I know not, the way is so dark	182
I KNOW THAT JESUS SAVES ME	101
I know that my Savior has found me	140
I'll praise thee, Savior	45
I LOVE TO TELL THE STORY	229
I'M SO GLAD THAT I LOVE JESUS	5
I now can sing Redemption's song	66
IN THE BY AND BY	189
In the dawning of the morning, when	191
In the face of sin and wrong	179
In the furrows of thy life	14
IN THE SUNSHINE	13
I SHALL BE SATISFIED	110
I shall hear the song that the	30
ISHI	195
I sought the Savior in my grief	170
I STRETCH MY HANDS TO THEE	224
I've looked my life over and	184
I WANT TO KNOW MORE	38
I was a wandering sheep	98
I was out on life's ocean, where	150

J

	No.
Jesus bids us shine with a bright	142
JESUS, HIDE ME	169
JESUS IS CALLING	154
JESUS IS CALLING TO-DAY	53
JESUS IS MINE	223
JESUS LEADS THE WAY	82
JESUS LOVES ALL	25
JESUS, MY ALL	233
Jesus, my all to heaven is gone	111
Jesus, Savior, pilot me	219
JESUS, THE CHILDREN'S FRIEND	107
JESUS, THE LIFE-BOAT	184
Jesus, when he left the sky	125
Joyfully now our hearts are	131
JOYFULLY SING	131
JUST ASK HIM IN TO STAY	89
JUST BEYOND THE RIVER	69

K

	No.
KEEP STEP IN THE MARCH	6
KEEP THE LIGHT OF JESUS SHINING	91
KING OF KINGS AND LORD OF LORDS	34
KNOCKING AT THE DOOR	3

L

	No.
LEIGHTON	208
LET JESUS HOLD YOUR HAND	23
LET US ARISE	18
Let us rally, rally, rally	28
Let us work for the Lord	164
LIFTING AS WE CLIMB	64
LIFT UP YOUR HEADS	178
LIFT UP YOUR HEARTS	72
LITTLE CANDLES	92
Little feet, be very careful	134
LITTLE ONES	125
LITTLE PILGRIMS	151
LIVING IN CANAAN	90
Long ago the Savior bought me	194
Lord of the living harvest	96
Lo! the blessed Savior stands	3
LOVE OF GOD	97
LOYAL AND TRUE	50

M

	No.
Make haste, O man, to live	208
MARCHING HOME	59
MARCHING TO ZION	230

INDEX

Title	No.
Marching with Jesus	52
Mercy for All	117
Mid scenes of confusion and creature	181
More Love to Thee	137
Morning, Noon, and Evening	149
Must Jesus Bear the Cross	228
My body, soul, and spirit	225
My country 't is of thee	210
My happy heart is free from sin	86
My heart is filled with joy to-day	101
My Home is Not Here	173
My Jesus, as Thou Wilt	209
My Jesus, I Love Thee	202
My soul, lift up thy voice	43

N

Title	No.
Nearer, My God	238
Nearer to Jesus	42
Nearer to thee, my Savior	137
No More a Wandering Sheep	98
Now let us sing the angels' song	8
Now, the sowing and the reaping	76

O

Title	No.
O bless the Lord for perfect peace	16
O brother, come out of the land	118
O Day of Rest and Gladness	222
O for a Heart	153
O for a heart to praise my God	58
O soldier brave, in strength	32
O the New, Bright Clime	57
O thou shelter from the tempest	169
O'er the trackless deep the sailor sails	180
Oh, for a Clean Heart	112
Oh, for a heart of devotion	112
Oh, for a heart to praise my God	216
Oh, how faithful is the saying	168
Oh, my heart is full of laughter	195
Oh, pilgrim, art thou weary	71
Oh, theme of blest salvation	48
Oh, think of the home over there	237
Oh, what boundless love we see	1
Once five tiny little seeds	124
On the Heavenly Way	41
On the highway of the King	84
On the Rock	60
On to Victory	44
Onward, Christian	19
Onward, Christian Soldier	20
Our Banner	31
Our Father which art in heaven	51, 127
Our hearts are light and cheerful	89

P

Title	No.
Power in Jesus' Blood	47
Praise Him	21
Praise the Lord. By Henry	8
Praise the Lord. By Myers	46
Praise the Lord. By Henry	81
Praise the Lord. By Gabriel	191
Praise the Rock of our salvation	21

R

Title	No.
Rallying Song	28
Remember Thy Creator	148
Remember, my boy, thy Creator	148
Resting on His Word	86
Rest, Soldier, Rest	190
Return, O Wanderer	167
Rock of Ages	211
Room for All	215

S

Title	No.
Safe on the Rock	68
Safe with Thee	113
Salvation! Oh, the joyful sound	217
Savior, Go with Me	197
Savior, Pilot Me	219
Scatter Golden Grain	10
Scatter Seed	14
Seeking Treasures	128
See the morning sunlight brighten	15
Seven Times Round	186
Shall I tell you why I sing a joyful lay	144
Shall We Meet	183
Shine, Shine, Shine	142
Shout the Tidings	85
Since Jesus Dwells Within	66
Since My Soul is Redeemed	166
Sing Joyfully, Sing Cheerily	177
Sing the Good Tidings of Mercy	30
Sinner, go; will you go	207
Sleep, soldier, take thy rest	190
Soldiers of Christ	32
Something to be Done	26
Song of Triumph	138
Sound it Out with Singing	187
Source of Every Blessing	114
Sowing and Reaping	55
Standing on the Rock of Ages	60
Stand up for Jesus	193
Sun of my soul, thou Savior dear	161
Sunshine by and by	152
Sweet Name of Jesus	145

T

Title	No.
Take the Name of Jesus	221
Tell it All to Jesus	141
Tell it to Jesus	234
Tell the Story	4
The Ark of His Love	118
The Beacon of Light	150
The Beautiful River	104
The Bridegroom Cometh	36
The bugle has sounded	52
The Christian Soldier	87
The Discontented Seeds	124
The Firm Foundation	218
The Glad Good News	24
The Great Mediator	2
The Harbor Lights of Home	180
The head that once was crowned	34
The Home Over There	237

INDEX

Title	No.
The King's Highway	84
The Life, the Truth, the Way	135
The Light of the Cross	120
The Lily of the Valley	235
The Lord's my shepherd, I'll not	56
The Lord's Prayer	51, 127
The Master's Call	130
The Master Comes	99
The morning light is breaking	119
The Music of the Kingdom	196
The Reaper May Call To-Night	105
The silver chord is loosened	157
The Sinner Invited	207
The Sure Refuge	54
The Sweet Olden Story	22
The thunders of judgment shall	123
The Voice of Praise	63
The Way of the Cross	139
Thee We Praise	83
There are clouds, but high above	152
There is a Happy Land	29
There is a name I love to hear	145
There is a safe and secret place	54
There's a battle to be fought	26
There's a beautiful river	104
There's a city bright and fair	69
There's a joyful message written in	2
There's a land beyond the sea	172
There's a stranger knocking at your	174
There is great rejoicing in my soul	68
There's power in Jesus' blood	47
There's room in God's eternal love	215
There will be singing and great	180
There Yet is Room	75
This Note Shall Swell	45
Thou Thinkest, Lord, of Me	203
Though Your Sins be as Scarlet	7
Thy Kingdom Come	96
Thy way, O God, is best	200
Thy Will be Done	201
'Tis a reasonable service	78
'Tis chill on the mountain of sin	126
'Tis Jesus Saves Me	133
'Tis the time of sowing, and the day	10
Toilers in the Vineyard	74
To the Christian legions comes the	4
Turn Thee, Brother	49
Trust It All with Jesus	71

U

Title	No.
Unending Praise	80

V

Title	No.
Victory is Coming	79

W

Title	No.
Waiting, Watching, Working	100
Walking in the Highway	129
Watching by the Cross	1
We are but little candles	92
We are here to gather jewels	128
We are Jesus' little ones	25
We are little pilgrims	151
We are Little Soldiers	62
We are marching under the banner	138
We are singing, ever singing	196
We are toiling on, oft in barren	55
We are waiting, waiting for the	100
We are willing workers in the	116
We live in the present, and not in the	160
We love to sing of Jesus	107
We Reap What We Sow	160
We Will Follow Thee	37
We will lift on high our banner	31
We're little Christian soldiers	93
We're soldiers in the army of the	87
Webb	119
What a Friend	232
What You Will Find in Jesus	136
When I think of my home in the	173
When the Gates of Heav'n Unfold	39
When the Mighty Trump	123
When the morning sun is bright	88
When the Roll is Called	106
When the skies are blue above our	177
When the trumpet of the Lord	106
When thy heart, with sin oppressing	155
When your heart is troubled	141
Where the harvest waves the fields	40
While there's little seed for me	50
While you onward fare, in the narrow	186
Who'll be a Soldier	132
Why idle rest the hands to-day	130
Why should I fear, when my Savior	67
Willing Workers	116
Wilt thou hear the voice of praise	63
Will You Go	172
With an everlasting love, came the	24
Won't You Let Him In	174
Work for the Lord	164
Work for the Night	192
Would you mount temptation's wave	33
Would You See Jesus	158

Y

Title	No.
Yes, I will bless thee, O my God	80
Ye toilers in the vineyard	74
Ye virgin souls, arise	171

Z

Title	No.
Zion Triumphant	146

www.ingramcontent.com/pod-product-compliance
Lightning Source LLC
Chambersburg PA
CBHW021844230426
43669CB00008B/1070